The Beginner's Guide to Office Boxing

The How-To's of Workplace Self-Defense

Paula Schumacher
in collaboration with Sirrka Heikenen

UpMesa Publishing

Copyright © 2012 Paula Schumacher

All rights reserved.

Blog: officeboxing.blogspot.com
eBook: http://www.smashwords.com/books/view/136473

Interior art by Marty Olson
Cover by Jud Kite, www.killerkite.com

ISBN-10: 0615606873
ISBN-13: 978-0615606873

CONTENTS

Foreword	v
Preface	vii
How to Use this Book	ix
Acknowledgments	xi
Introduction	1
Training	5
Basic Skills	11
Opponents	19
Alexander "the Great"	21
Faith "the Phantom"	29
Katy "the Chaos Kid"	37
Sam "the Saboteur"	45
Stella "the Belle"	55
Conrad "the Con Man"	63
Mark "the Machine"	73
Nora "the Needy Gnat"	81
Gil "the Nice Guy"	89
Lloyd "the Paranoid Pounder"	95
Boxing Hierarchy	105
Historic Boxing Rules	107
Glossary of Terms	111
Resources	115

FOREWORD

Michael Marley

I've been involved in boxing so long that some claim I was in the press section when Cain and Abel went twelve rounds or less. I have been around big-time boxing a half century now. I started as a starry-eyed kid whose idol was Cassius Clay, who became Muhammad Ali. I got to meet the champ of all champs as a teenager, and since then, boxing has been my business in one form or another: as a boxing columnist (New York Post), TV producer (for Howard Cosell), as a minister of "misinformation" (for controversial Don King, who had a controversial cash cow named Mike Tyson), and as a lawyer and manager of several world champions.

Those of us in the "fight game" have an expression about outsiders and wannabes who pretend to know our business and sport: "Freddy—he doesn't know a left hook from a fish hook!" Which brings me to the slugging junior lightweight from Kansas named Paula J. Schumacher. To continue with boxing lingo, she fights above her weight in this serious but humorous tome.

I say this book is useful for anyone who has a job, has ever had a job, or ever hopes to have a job again. Even those lucky dogs who are comfortably retired will benefit. People will laugh and cry when they read about Ms. Schumacher's insightful and witty delineations of the "types" of fighters you will find working alongside you at a donut shop, a hospital, a big mall store, a college, or your local widget factory. (Oh, my bad ... I forgot—all the widget shops are in the Philippines and likely owned by current boxing "king" Manny Pacquiao.) But the appeal of and the value of this creative work is not limited to the workplace. College students, high school kids, and even those in junior high can identify and relate to such venomous classmates/competitors as those in our workplaces that the author has described.

Ms. Schumacher gives advice great champs such as Sugar Ray Leonard or Ali can appreciate when she says sometimes you have to hug it out. Or, as we call it in the prize ring, clinching. Clinching is a great tactic, often the only sensible one, when you are tired or hurt. The office stereotypes she describes are hilarious but all have a ring—the ring of truth.

I zipped through this breezy book like Ali did when he made "Big Ugly Bear" Sonny Liston look like a housecat. And you will too. Buy a copy for yourself and one for each of your co-workers who are decent folks. It should be a lot of fun naming the fighters that you know and/or have worked with.

And, never forget what is perhaps the writer's best fight pointer: never, ever take your eyes off an opponent—especially a cretin like Conrad "the Con Man." As we say in boxing, it's the punch you never see that really hurts you.

PREFACE

Sirrka Heikenen, PhD, licensed psychologist

For over two decades I have worked with a wide range of individuals and businesses in various capacities. In my private practice I have met countless people who have reached, or even passed, their last hope of enduring within their dysfunctional work setting. Their clinical symptoms range from severe anxiety and prolonged panic attacks to true clinical depression. Of course we all emerge into adulthood as the sum total of our life experiences. However, the emotional and physical suffering of the persons to whom I refer can be directly traced to their attempts to endure severe and dysfunctional workplace situations.

Workplace dysfunction is frequently approached as a systems problem, which as far as it goes is accurate. But if we take this analysis a step deeper, systemic problems can typically be traced to specific dysfunctional people. While all of us carry our own "normal" range of problems and peculiarities, I am referring here to a much more toxic, severe, and entrenched type of personality. Mental health experts and diagnostic manuals refer to these persons as personality disordered. In my own career assessments of workplace problems, I would attribute at least seventy-five percent of both the tangible and intangible human suffering within such workplace settings to such personality-disordered individuals.

Often these individuals are in positions of authority over co-workers, but that is not always the case. Personality-disordered individuals might also be fellow office mates or persons we supervise. Whatever the case, the predictable outcome will be an erosion of workplace harmony, and the resulting human suffering is immeasurable. I am referring to the damage done to people who have invested their own considerable time and resources to become good at their jobs and experts in their fields. These are typically the people who do their best to be team players, to adhere to whatever corporate model is in place, to believe in their companies and what they stand for—and they believe other employees do as well.

My attitudes and opinions about these types of workplace situations have developed from my perspective as a clinical psychologist assessing personal and systemic dynamics from the outside-in. I consider Paula Schumacher to have become a corporate systems expert from the inside-out. For over a decade, we have spent countless hours analyzing and discussing the underpinnings of such workplace dysfunction to help each other understand and articulate the difference between a "normal" and therefore tolerable, possibly even solvable, workplace problem and the deeper and more malignant problems created by personality-disordered persons within the workplace. In the latter situation, when in a situation we may not be able to alter or change, the only real solution is to develop survival skills. I agree with Paula that within this specific workplace context, knowing how to apply the rules of office boxing to specific personality-disordered persons can be a life-saver. Certainly it can be a mental health saver.

Paula's considerable experience with workplace dynamics is impressive. But I have found her ability to understand and translate these often confusing dynamics into clear and understandable book form to be nothing short of remarkable. I have used this book in numerous situations and with numerous clients representing a wide spectrum of businesses and difficult situations. The feedback I have received has been overwhelmingly positive. The first response has often been surprise, even shock, that someone actually understands their work situation. And in learning that there are options even within these toxic environments, my clients have frequently expressed tremendous relief, hope, and even healing. I certainly believe this book will be instructive and helpful to business employees and other mental health professionals. But I would also like to imagine this book being read by every employee in every human resources department, as it would simplify and offer constructive options to ameliorate the most serious and, unfortunately, many of the most frequent complaints HR professionals encounter.

HOW TO USE THIS BOOK

For a quick fix, use this flowchart to determine which opponent you are facing and then jump to that chapter. If the fighter profile doesn't seem to be a match to your opponent, back up a step in the flow chart and see if the next closest fighter is a match. Reading the book from front to back will give you a "train, then fight" experience.

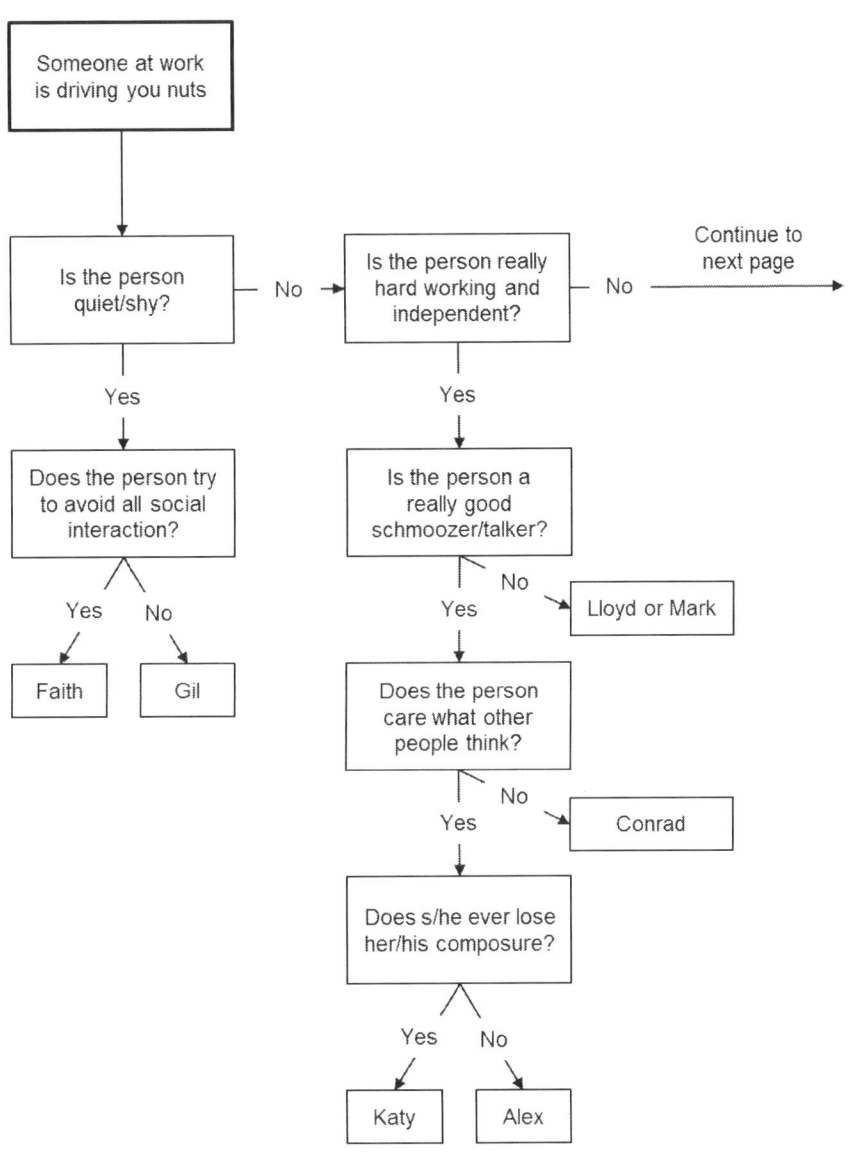

Paula Schumacher

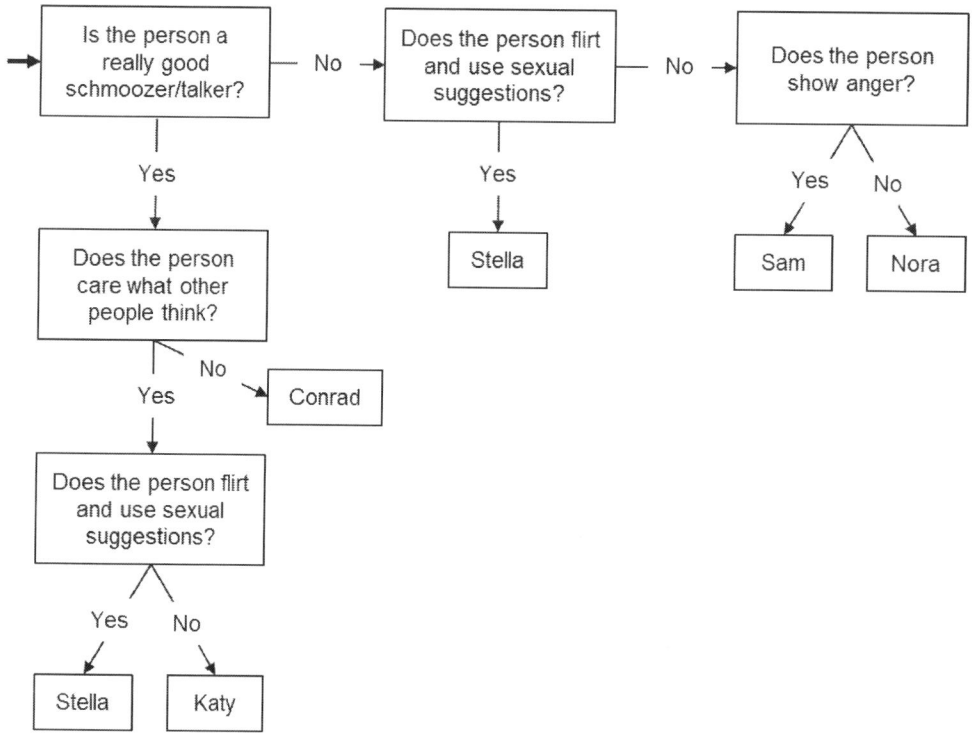

Note: Some fighters are erratic in their personalities, and some are putting on an act. Sometimes you need to watch them closely, get input from others, etc., before you know enough to determine which opponent they are.

ACKNOWLEDGMENTS

Paula Schumacher

First and foremost, hearty thanks to Sirrka "the Velvet Hammer" Heikenen. You helped me learn the science of office boxing and were always in my corner. Linda Gwaltney: I couldn't have done this without your unconditional support. Carol Aydelott: your sharing and love have been more than wonderful—you are the best sister ever. Thanks to everyone who pitched in with stories, reviews, boxing lingo, and encouragement. Marty "the Painted Bear" Olson, you did an amazing job capturing the images of the fighters. Finally: Denise. If you hadn't given me such a whipping in the work place, I never would have been so wounded as to finally try to figure all this out.

Sirrka Heikenen

I owe my deepest gratitude to Paula Schumacher. I can be quite passionate, some might even say "unstoppable," in my desire to communicate to "normal" people the dangers of personality disordered individuals. Out of the volumes of information I have provided, Paula has been able to distill out the essential basic information into this book covering introductory material about Personality Disordered persons in the workplace.

No words can express the thanks and admiration I have for the many patients who have worked through the difficult situations described in this book. I thank them for allowing me to share their experiences that helped in the development of the case examples at the end of each chapter.

★ ★ ★ INTRODUCTION ★ ★ ★

Why You Need to Know How to Fight in the Office

No matter what management or business guru you've studied or read, once you've been in an office environment for a few years, it becomes painfully obvious that it's an eat-or-be-eaten world. No matter what "play nice together" policy your company posts or your manager assures you is in place, the dysfunctions people have do not stay at home—they come to work with each of us.

If you just can't seem to break through to the next level, or you are a nice person who finds yourself out of a job when you know you do good work, or the credit for your work is too often taken by another, then in the office you are the equivalent of a ninety-pound weakling. Learn to box—learn to protect yourself and your work. The goal of this guide is not to make you into a bully who gets into slugfests with other bullies but to help you develop into a boxer: a fighter with cool judgment, ring savvy, and effective strategy, in addition to a bag full of tricks.

A Bit about the History of Boxing

Fist fighting for sport dates back six thousand years to Africa. From Africa it spread to the Mediterranean, where the Greeks added it to their gladiator amusements. It was a brutal sport: two matched fighters sat facing each other, trading blows, until one died. The leather straps fighters used to protect their hands evolved into studded and spurred weapons under the Romans. The Romans are also credited with inventing the ring, which was a drawn circle. As Christianity rose in popularity, boxing declined. Christian Roman emperors Constantine and Theodoric eliminated boxing from gladiatorial combat.

In the seventeenth century, boxing resurfaced in England, where it gained respectability and rules. Broughton's Rules (listed in the appendix) came first in 1743, followed by the London Prize Ring Rules around 1814, making boxing a sport where the goal was to defeat, not kill, the opponent. Broughton also introduced boxing gloves, but only to protect the face and hands in practice bouts. Actual boxing matches were still generally forbidden in England. With the advent of the Marquis of Queensberry Rules (listed in the appendix) in 1867, the authorities began to allow the sport. Legitimized, boxing began to flourish.

The Rules of Office Boxing

Like the rules of the boxing sport, the rules in the business arena have evolved. They are affected by conditions outside the sport, such as industrial, economic, and social conditions. People within the sport (such as business owners and managers) have latitude in determining what rules are to be used, bent, and ignored. Although there are no standards, you can generally go by these basic office boxing rules and modify them for to suit your particular office.

1. Learn the posted rules. Every organization has posted rules for how employees interact, how business is conducted, etc. You can usually find these in orientation packets, business mottos and slogans, professional ethics handouts, process documents, and at employee meetings. Always keep the posted rules in mind, and try to follow them to the letter, if not the intent, when possible.

2. Learn the "gym" rules. These rules are set by your direct manager or supervisor. The nature of gym rules is that they vary, and they are not posted because they are not technically legal. If your manager comes under pressure from above, he may revert to the posted rules and bust you for breaking them—even though you were okay following his rules the week before. Because of this, it is also good to learn the gym rules of your manager's manager.

Example: The posted rules state employees need to request vacation leave two weeks in advance. Your manager is more relaxed and will let you off with just a few days notice if you can show him everything will be covered in your absence. You know your co-worker Rita, who's fallen out of favor with your manager, has to have her requests turned in a month in advance.

---

3. Know yourself. As much as possible, learn your strengths and weaknesses—and quantify them. When your boss complains about your work, do you know if it is really that bad? Or is she just using you as a punching bag to vent her frustration? Your opponents will look for your weaknesses and avoid your strengths. You need to know yourself better than your opponent does to have a fighting chance.

> **Tip:** If you don't have healthy self-esteem, you probably judge yourself too harshly. This plays to your opponent's advantage: she hits you once, and then you continue hitting yourself for her.

4. Stay alert. Each and every person is a potential opponent. There are many forces that move us to act. You never know when job security, the possibility of a raise, or the need to be perfect in another's eyes will turn a friend into an opponent. You can make friends at work; just be careful how close you let them in. Since everyone in the office is a potential opponent, it is possible that you may find an enemy in your corner. The person giving you advice may be having lunch with your opponent on a regular basis. If you find this to be the case, keep a cool head. Take advice, weigh it well, and fight the best you can. Don't ever rely completely on another person.

5. Never tell your opponent that you have a glass jaw. If you have to disclose a weakness at work (maybe you need to learn a skill you don't have), do so in such a way that others see you improving a skill, not filling a void.

6. Don't take fights personally. You're a fighter, your opponent is a fighter, you fight—that's life. Don't forget what happens, but let it go. If you take trash talking and fighting personally, your anger will cloud your ability to think, and you won't be able to fight as well. Should you be angry? Is it okay to be angry? Hell, yes! Just not at work.

7. There's more than one way to fight. Every communication, whether written, electronic, or face-to-face, is a potential punch. Be careful what you say; you don't want to swing wildly or punch someone by mistake. Don't ignore trash talk—those are jabs, and they can do real damage.

8. Be prepared to go the distance. Office boxing matches don't have a set number of rounds, very few fights end in a knockout, and rematches are plentiful.

★ ★ ★ TRAINING ★ ★ ★

Just like a boxer, you'll do better in the ring if you are in shape. Here are some basic exercises for office boxing. Begin slowly, and find a workout partner if you can. Don't get discouraged if you don't see immediate results; getting in good office boxing shape takes more effort than getting in good physical shape.

Road Work

Running builds endurance. A boxer gets a lot of his conditioning from road work. He will often run a mile for each round he expects to fight in an upcoming match. The boxer runs on the balls of his feet and breathes only through his nose—just like he will in the fight. In office boxing, road work is very different. You build up your endurance by reducing stress in as many areas of your life as possible. Take care of your physical and mental health, and you'll last longer in the ring.

Take up a hobby that interests you, even if you can't give it all the attention you'd like. Find something that helps you relax, and incorporate it into your daily life. And exercise. Some hobbies (such as hiking or golf) help you both relax and exercise.

One advantage that road work will give you in office boxing is another life. Some office boxers see work as everything. They have no outside interests and think that a loss in the ring would be the end of their career and, therefore, their life. While this gives them a lot of heart to fight hard, they're burning themselves out. If you are fulfilled in other areas of your life and know you could find another job, then you have a weapon a lot of people don't realize they have: you can walk away.

Stretching

Stretching provides flexibility. Flexibility means you can roll with the punches better. Get in the habit of stretching your skills and acquaintances. You never know when a skill, even one as simple as clearing jams from a photocopier, can win you points with one of the judges. Knowing a judge personally—even if it's a relationship that only lasts an elevator ride a day—can also win you points. Don't forget your co-workers. They're the shouting crowd at ringside. It's always good to have some of them rooting for you.

Stretching can help improve your mobility. A mobile boxer usually gets hit less than one standing flat-footed in the ring. An office boxer who's done her stretching and has passing acquaintances with her upper management, peers, and subordinates will have more people in her corner, rooting for her to win, when it's fight time.

Stretching your circle of work friends can be as easy as joining a conversation about how the local sports team is doing or the plot of a popular TV show (avoid politics and religion). Usually you can tell what his interests are by the items a person keeps on his desk. Some office boxers take affront at being asked about their family life. Avoid more personal topics until you know your co-workers better.

Tip: Don't expect the crowd to back you. Crowds root for whoever they perceive to be the more powerful fighter. It doesn't matter if you're in the right, if you're the victim, or even if you're the manager: if your opponent looks stronger, the crowd is on his side. If you win, the crowd will shift to align itself with you.

Jumping Rope

Jumping rope helps a boxer develop footwork and coordination. It's also a great cardiovascular workout. Boxing is physically demanding. A boxer tries to get in peak condition so he isn't fighting against his own body as well as his opponent in the ring. The office boxer has to get in good mental shape.

If someone comes up to you and berates you or your work and you find your face getting hot, tears welling, your breath changing, or your fists clenching, then you are not in good mental shape. You need to build up your defense so you aren't easily rattled. This isn't blocking emotions; it's learning how to think and then act instead of just reacting. Hold the situation up for inspection and decide whether to use your emotion or intellect, or both.

The next time you feel you are under attack, take a moment to observe before you respond. In that moment, you may notice what the weather is like, what time it is, what color shirt your opponent is wearing. As you continue working with this exercise, you will be able to notice several things without the other person realizing you aren't fully engaged. And you will realize that you have achieved distance. They are talking and you are listening—but you are also able to think. Take a breath of air.

This distance serves as a type of boundary: they can't get into your thoughts, your head. You have a safety zone, at least enough distance to consider what is happening. You have enough time to make a quick gut-check on their accusations and think about where they are coming from and come to a decision about how you will react.

> **Example:** Rita says, "You're always late to work."
>
> Fred does a mental check. "Am I? Today and once last week, but I'm always on time otherwise." And "She's angry because she had to chat with my client, who showed up early." And "I'm going to address the real issue of her not liking to deal with clients."

This exercise is difficult to learn, but the benefits it provides are worth it. First, the distance provides you with a buffer so attacks don't seem to be directly in your face. Second, with the buffer and your thoughts, you can weed out what issue is yours and what is your opponent's. Third, the more accurate your perceptions of your opponents, the better you understand them and the better you can counter—or avoid the situation in the future. All of the benefits of jumping rope help reduce stress and give you a feeling of personal control—which helps keep your emotions from being easily triggered.

> **Tip:** Don't forget to get your feelings out. Exercise, relaxation, and especially talking it out with a friend are good ways to vent emotions.

Shadow Boxing

Shadow boxing is one of the best exercises boxers use to improve their skills. Each day boxers spend at least twenty minutes in front of a mirror boxing with their reflection. As they throw jabs, crosses, hooks, and uppercuts in different combinations, boxers adjust their form and tighten their defense.

This exercise translates to one thing for the office boxer: practice fights. You need to get used to remaining calm and balanced in the face of attacks. You want your body to reflect the calmness of your mind. And you want to know what to say in the heat of the moment—not three days later at home. You need practice.

Watch and listen to how more advanced fighters handle punches, and try it out yourself. Use visualization to re-enact fights in your mind and imagine different outcomes. Get a friend to practice exchanges with you. Stand in front of a mirror and pretend your reflection is your opponent. Have a fight. Practice responses. Block insults and counter with facts. And through it all, check your attitude. Are you taking things personally? Do you have distance? Is your facial expression calm?

Like all the other exercises, it will take time for you to become comfortable shadow boxing—and more time for you to see improvement.

Tip: Get in plenty of shadow boxing, and begin a little sparring outside of work, where the stakes aren't so high. Don't pick fights; just defend yourself when you find yourself in one. For example, if someone cuts into the line at the grocery store or bank, point it out to the person, as well as everyone else in line. Don't get into a real fight over it, but don't let them just sneak in without an apology or excuse.

Diet

A boxer's diet tends to be low in rich, fried, and fatty foods. While a diet of compliments and fans might increase a boxer's confidence and give him momentum in a match, too much makes him overconfident and sloppy. Accept compliments, awards, and raises, but don't let them go to your head. No certificate on the wall ever stopped a bully from pummeling an easy victim. Remember that fans have their own reasons for being in your camp. They may like your style. They may like you more than your opponent. Or they may have some money riding on whether you fight, win, or lose.

Take all feedback (positive and negative) seriously but objectively. Weigh its accuracy concerning yourself, and consider what it says about the person who gave it to you. If you aren't getting any feedback, use your stretching skills or go directly to your manager to find out why.

Example: Toni is proud of herself for reformatting the status report. She halved the time it will take to complete it. She is surprised she hasn't heard anything from her boss, Gerald, who is big on process improvements. When she catches him in his office and asks about it, she is surprised to hear management hates it. She takes a calming breath and asks what they hate about it. Gerald tells her it was too much of a change without warning. And because Toni didn't forewarn him, he wasn't able to defend it. Toni and Gerald continue talking and figure out a way to reintroduce the changes in a more structured, moderate process.

Sleep

When boxers are in training, they work their bodies hard and then increase sleep time to allow their bodies to heal and strengthen. If you aren't used to the fight life, getting in good office boxing shape will probably put your emotions through a tough workout and leave you physically drained. Give yourself more relaxation and sleep time during training.

★ ★ ★ BASIC SKILLS ★ ★ ★

Even if you plan to never throw a punch, it's helpful to know what one looks like and how it's used. The same goes for defensive moves. Awareness is half the battle.

Stance

The boxer's stance coordinates the entire body, from the balls of the feet to the tilt of the head, for optimal fight results. Everything is related to the way he holds his body: mobility, defense, and offense. If he's heavy on his feet, he loses mobility. If his stance is too open or closed, his opponent will be able to easily land punches on him. If his arms aren't positioned correctly, he can't be as effective blocking and delivering punches.

The way you hold yourself physically and mentally defines your stance in the office environment. If you look weak, you invite a punch. If you look strong, people will think twice before attacking you. If your mind is dull and slow to react, your opponent will know she can beat you to the punch. If your mind is sharp and you react quickly, your opponent will learn he can't land punches on you without leaving himself open to your counterpunches.

Refine your body language until you feel comfortable presenting an aura of confidence in both neutral and stressful situations. Stance includes knowing your work and your facts. Be well-grounded in your knowledge, so when you're trading blows, you know your punches are verifiable facts.

Punches

The jab is one of the first punches a boxer learns to throw. A jab comes off your lead hand and is used to gauge distance and keep your opponent off balance. Boxers also use the jab at the beginning and end of combinations to set up other punches, provide partial defense, and bring themselves back into balance. You know what a jab feels like from the receiving end: someone nickel and dimes you with assignments to see how much you'll put up with. Your jab will be different. It will tell your opponent, "This is my space, that's yours." Some sample jabs are:

- Not accepting an unfair or incorrect review of your work.

- Going home when you have a personal commitment instead of staying late yet again to meet another deadline in a long line of deadlines.
- Refusing to do someone else's work unless there is a good reason, management is aware of your extra effort, and you will be compensated in some way.
- Requesting comparable pay for comparable work.

Combined with jump-rope training (see Training), your jab helps you gather information about the type of opponent facing you. Watch how your opponent reacts to your jab. Is it always the same reaction? If so, you can plan how to take advantage of it if needed.

Example: Bette's office receptionist, Sharon, is so vindictive she'll let orders go unfilled just to get back at staff. Bette has battled Sharon several times and knows Sharon will always call in sick if Bette asks her to catch up on the filing. Bette can use Sharon's standard reaction to either "make" Sharon be absent on cue (alerting management to watch for the problem) or set it up so Sharon can't take her usual escape.

Make sure people buy your jab. If your jab doesn't have any power to it, people will notice and start to ignore it. Put something into it, and people will respect it.

The cross, or straight right (straight left if you're left-handed) is a power punch. Once you've jabbed around a bit and know who and where your opponent is, use this punch for serious damage when it's time for some heavy hitting. Some pointers about the cross:

- Aim through your target. When you throw this punch, give it all you've got—no holding back. Present your case with all your facts carefully laid out so there's no question your opponent is in the wrong. This punch is not a wake-up call to let them know you're upset; it's a knock-their-lights-out punch because they've stepped way over the line.

- Keep your hands (defenses) up. There's nothing to stop your opponent from hitting you at the same time you're hitting him. Be prepared for your opponent to bring up issues about you, or even say you are responsible for the very thing you're accusing him of.

- Don't telegraph. Don't let someone know you're going to hit him. Sharing your strategy with an office mate, giving your opponent a warning (other than a jab), or trash talking let your opponent know you are about to punch him, which gives him time to set up his defense or counterattack.

A good cross would include proving an employee to be incompetent or unprofessional, using facts.

Example: Jack expects his co-worker Toni to be his secretary. He also wants to date her and sends her e-mails that are very unprofessional. Toni has told Jack she isn't his secretary and isn't interested in dating. No matter how many times Toni defines her space with jabs, Jack ignores the warnings. Toni meets with her boss about the situation. He's not totally convinced there's a problem. Toni forwards Jack's e-mails and other proof she's collected and reminds the boss about the company sexual harassment policy. Jack is out like a light.

Hooks are harder to deliver but are worth working on because your opponent doesn't usually see them coming. In the office, your hooks are set up either so the blow doesn't come directly from you, or is on a topic that your opponent thinks you agree on. Don't overextend on this punch or throw wild punches—that leaves you wide open for a counterpunch.

Example: Bette's co-worker stole her client. Bette has a chance to get the client back from Janet only if Janet blows the initial consultation. Bette learns the meeting is tomorrow and also hears Janet asking Sharon (the receptionist) to get a dossier ready for her. Bette tells Sharon that the filing is behind and needs to be worked on, knowing full well that Sharon will react by taking a sick day. Sharon takes ill, and Bette's hook hits hard when Janet can't get the dossier together in time for her meeting.

Uppercuts are great for infighting. When you're in a clinch or have your opponent on the ropes, use uppercuts to pound his body and weaken his resolve. Use whatever you have in your arsenal to drive your point home. In the office, these punches are like airing all the dirty laundry. Be careful to avoid illegal and dangerous blows. Your opponent is on the ropes, but he can still come back.

> **Example:** Although Jack was caught out for sexual harassment, his boss liked him and wanted to keep him on in a different role. The boss appealed to Toni for leniency in pressing her charges. Toni said she could think it over, but she told her boss she had heard of two other women with similar complaints about Jack and was concerned for the company's reputation if they kept him. She added that Jack boasted to her about using the company's money for personal vacations—possibly another reason to rethink keeping Jack.

Keep these points in mind about your punches:

- You may have the power to hit hard, but landing a punch may injure you as well as your opponent. Be aware that in the eyes of your peers and management there are consequences to being seen as aggressive. You should always have good cause for being in the fight and for throwing your punches.

- Mix up your punches so you don't become predictable. Avoid reacting the same way again and again.

- Watch how your opponent reacts to your punches. This will help you land more follow-up punches and remind you to keep your defenses up. For example, in a real fight, boxers know that if they get an uppercut in, their opponent's head tends to move up and their arms out, which is a perfect situation to try a hook.

Defense

A good boxer knows that the fight is about not getting hit as much as it is about hitting. To avoid punches, first you need to see them coming: don't take your eyes off your opponent. Everyone has a natural tendency to flinch or close their eyes when they are about to get hit. Boxers learn to overcome this reaction and keep their opponent in sight at all times. When the punch does come, you have three choices: let it hit you, block it, or try to avoid it all together.

Letting a punch land on you (as opposed to not seeing it) is more strategy than defense. You might allow a punch in because it allows you an opportunity to counterpunch when your opponent is most vulnerable. Or you may allow it in order to feel the pain and then use that as motivation to fight back. I don't recommend this technique for beginners. You need to know what damage the punch will do, whether you can sustain that damage and continue, and if you can leverage the blow to your advantage—all of which requires a good understanding of your opponent, yourself, and the venue.

If you choose to block the punch, use the basic blocking technique of meeting the punch with your glove or arm. The hand you block with won't be free to counterpunch. In other words, you allow the attack, but you don't let it all the way in and you don't hit back.

Example: Rita tells Fred (in front of others or privately) that the meeting minutes from last week were in the wrong format. Fred knows he followed the format that Rita gave him, but he doesn't want to get into a fight there and then. He says, "I followed my notes from our last discussion about minutes, but maybe I didn't get all of your instructions down." Then he asks what she would like changed and whether she'd like him to redistribute the minutes.

- Fred does not apologize.
- Fred is careful not to be sarcastic or do anything to inflame Rita.

You can roll with the punch by yielding to the blow to take the sting out of it. You let your opponent's punch land because you know how to take it so it doesn't hurt you.

Example: In a busy hallway, Rita pulls Fred aside and tells him he isn't dressed appropriately. Fred knows Rita has a thing about sweater vests, but there is no rule against them, and other employees wear them. He says, "Oh, yeah, I do look a little too casual today."

- Fred does not apologize.
- Fred is not sarcastic and doesn't try to inflame Rita.
- Fred doesn't take off the vest. (And he probably wears it again after a couple of months.)

When your opponent is overwhelming, you can cover up. Boxers on the ropes will hunch over, protect their face and body with their arms as best they can, and weather the storm. While you are covering up, try to remember that, on average, a person has only enough energy to support an outburst for a few minutes. With more fuel (input from you or co-workers) they can go longer. So try not to feed their anger—be as quiet as possible. Listen to their arguments and make notes of inconsistencies and errors that you may be able to use in your defense later.

When you are tired or hurt and need time to collect yourself, go into a clinch. In a boxing clinch, one fighter hugs his opponent (he's actually holding his arms to stop him from delivering blows and is resting his weight on him). The office clinch means going to your opponent's corner: praise her, compliment her, agree with her—anything to stop the punches and get some rest until you are recovered. When you're in a clinch, remember that it's still a fight situation. Avoid head butts, and watch for uppercuts.

Avoiding punches is harder than blocking punches. It requires quickness and good judgment. It's dangerous because if you miscalculate or are not fast enough, you get hit (usually in the head). Boxers avoid punches by slipping, ducking, and leaning away.

Example: Rita goes to Fred's desk and demands to know why he hasn't taken off the sweater vest. Fred says, "After we talked I met the CEO in passing, and he said he liked my vest—I didn't want to take it off and offend him."

- Fred does not apologize.
- Fred is not sarcastic and doesn't try to inflame Rita.

If an opponent comes at you with a barrage (fast, hard punches one after the other), as each punch is thrown, verify its validity. If it is not valid, or it is a gross distortion of one of your weaknesses, then your opponent is unconsciously belting you with his own weaknesses and fears. You can use this knowledge to throw counterpunches now or for building future strategies.

Example: Nolan is working on several projects with competing deadlines. He and his manager have a system in place for dealing with these situations, and Nolan is using that system. Nolan's busy, but he's making steady progress toward the deadlines and is feeling good. Peter, his manager, comes in and lets loose: "How's that Jones project coming along? Did you talk to Marci about the changes? How many hours will that set us back? I'm worried that's going to impact the Roberts project—how's that one coming along? I'd like a draft on that one today." Nolan takes a calming breath and does a quick mental check: is he doing what he should be doing? Is he on course? The answers are yes. Nolan relaxes a bit. When Peter finishes, Nolan says, "I'm working on the changes for Jones now. Everything is on track to meet deadline. Can I shoot you an e-mail or get with you in an hour to go over the specifics?" Peter says that would be fine.

- Nolan realizes that he is doing what he should be doing. In a time of calm, he and Peter agreed on the best strategy, and Nolan is following it. In the craziness of deadline pressure, Peter's fears about missing deadlines are coming out.

- Nolan speaks to Peter's fear (everything is on track to meet deadline) but doesn't give in to it by answering Peter's questions immediately. It would take him off track. Also, he knows from experience that if he does answer questions, Peter will come up with more. The best strategy is to buy time so he can finish up his current task; Peter gets a chance to calm down, and Nolan gets time to pull answers together.

When you're on defense:

- Always keep your eyes on your opponent.
- If you avoid a punch, try to make sure it doesn't land on someone else.

★ ★ ★ OPPONENTS ★ ★ ★

Here are the profiles of opponents you will encounter in the ring. These are profiles of the champions of each type. You will probably never run across an opponent who's as clear-cut as the ones here—your opponents will be a mixed bag. Some will have the same trainers or managers but not the same skills. Others will have a different reach or height. Whatever the difference, keep your focus and remember your skills.

Also remember it is extremely rare for a person to be conscious of the type of fighter they are. Everyone believes he or she is right and is acting normally. Show people the fighter profile that best matches them, and their reaction is confusion; show it to the people they work with, and you'll get a very different reaction.

WARNING: As you read about the opponents, you may find that you share some characteristics with them. This is normal: everyone has some of these characteristics to a degree. If you find you share all or almost all the characteristics of an opponent profiled here, you may wish to seek professional help.

Fighter profile descriptions are organized under these headings:

- Fighter Name: Fighter's name and nickname.
- Alias: Street name / psychological profile.
- Fight Record: How often fighters get what they want.
- Fight Division: The fighter's intensity, low (light) to high (heavy).
- Striking Reach: The fighter's ability to cause harm in various ways and through other people.
- Height: Where in the company's organization you would usually find the fighter.
- Manager: Which forces created the fighter.

- Fighter Profile: Typical identifying traits of the fighter.
- Defense: Tactics the fighter uses to defend him/herself.
- Offense: Tactics the fighter uses against others.
- Why Are You Fighting? Probable reasons why this fighter and you would get into an argument.
- In the Ring: Tips to keep in mind when you are in a fight with the fighter.
- Matchups: Tips to keep in mind if you are the fighter's boss, co-worker, or subordinate.
- Fight Commentaries: Examples of fights with the fighter (based on real-life situations).

★ ★ ★ ALEXANDER "THE GREAT" ★ ★ ★

Alias: The Exploiter, Narcissist.

Record: Seemingly perfect.

Division: Heavyweight.

Reach: Long.

Height: All levels of an organization, especially in upper management.

Manager: A core belief that his true self is not loveable has led this fighter to create a false perfect image.

Fighter Profile

Alex seems to be perfect. He's got the right moves, great combinations, and all the right people in his corner a guy could want. No punches seem to land on Alex—he's not a fighter who'll have cauliflower ears or a busted nose. Not only does Alex boast, he gets others to boast for him too. When Alex is doing the boasting, it will probably sound like a factual report or name dropping.

Sometimes when Alex is busy and you need something that he legitimately should provide, he may flick or elbow you (both are fouls), saying that you are too demanding, immature, selfish, etc., and you should be able to do it yourself. If you complain about his hyper-criticalness, he will say you are oversensitive.

Alex likes to take critical pokes at people. Sometimes his hits contain a grain of truth, but he really intends to make you take blame off his shoulders, not help you improve. Never underestimate his charm and ability to target your vulnerabilities. Alex is a predator who thrives on the office boxing life.

If you believe Alex is perfect and tell him so, you're in his corner. If you don't tell him how great he is, you're probably one of his punching bags. You're probably his punching bag either way—because if rumor of an imperfection lands anywhere near Alex, he's going to sucker you into taking the fall for all his mistakes and then put on a public show of cleaning up after you … thereby saving the day.

Don't be fooled by his superficiality; Alex is no cardboard-cutout fighter. Alex can be a very hard worker. He pushes himself hard and goes to the mat for the company. He will do almost anything to defend his title and get in good with upper management.

Defense

Alex's defense is his footwork. He never seems to be the reason the project went over budget, a deadline was missed, or the client got upset. He'll make it look like he's the one who helped the auditor find the budget oversight. He'll find a way to be part of the solution to the schedule issue and the champion of the day—not the loser. If the client was upset, Alex will find a scapegoat to take the punishment and then go golfing with the client. His footwork enables him to never take a firm stand on an issue until he knows which is the winning side. You might think you remember that Alex was the one with the now-sour idea, but Alex will point out that it was actually someone else.

You might notice that Alex never genuinely apologizes or thanks anybody. This backpedaling tactic helps him avoid imperfection (apologizing implies he's done something wrong, and thanking implies he needed help). It may make you feel as fuzzy-headed as someone who's just been knocked out. Listen to Alex's "apology" and see if he isn't actually:

- Stating his good intentions. "I meant to make it to the meeting, but traffic was so heavy I was too late."
- Baiting and switching. "Let me take you out for lunch."
- Explaining it all away. "Everyone opened and read their e-mail so fast that I couldn't yank it back and correct it."
- Sharing the love. "Jones may not like the report, but that's how you taught me to write reports."
- Overreaction. Too much of an apology may not be an apology at all—especially if you end up apologizing or reassuring Alex. "I can't believe I did that! I must be a rotten boss." (You're supposed to jump in and reassure him that he's okay.)

Alex is much better at being ungrateful than thankful. When it comes to a thank-you, this is about what you'll get:

- Approval. "You did a good job," instead of "Thank you for helping me meet the deadline."
- Role reversal. "Sure" or "Okay," to imply that you're the one with needs, when in fact you're the one who's just done something to help him.
- Refusal. "I don't deserve it" when you compliment him instead of simple acceptance. His response may make you feel like complimenting or reassuring him even more. A change-up of this tactic is when he thanks his staff, without whom he wouldn't have been able to accomplish so much. In effect he is taking all the credit for the work, giving some credit back to his staff, and getting you to admire him for sharing the credit.
- Overreaction. Alex may over-thank for the same reasons he may over-apologize. "You're a genius—we couldn't have done it without you" is not only an overreaction, it is also ring talk for "Guess who's doing this from now on?"

Offense

When it comes to ring survival skills, Alex's are the best. The higher up in the rankings Alex is, the more skills he has. The entourage he's built is in itself enough to defeat many would-be contenders. If you see a person in the office with a bunch of true-believer yes men around him, groupies who believe he walks on water, then you're looking at some of the people in Alex's corner. If you're in a fight with Alex, expect his entourage to come at you as well.

Alex is also good at beating people with their own fists. People have given Alex a training tip and come back wondering if they weren't the ones that needed to work on that skill.

Why Are You Fighting?

If you're lower in rank, you're defending yourself from getting blamed for something of his that didn't turn out. If you're higher in rank, you're trying to get him to face up to something he's done—or keep him from going after your own position. If you're the same rank, it can be for either reason. If you're not sure why you're fighting, you did or said something that he took as an attack on his character, and he is now merely defending himself.

In the Ring

When you find yourself in the ring with Alex, you have two options: flatter him or knock him flat. If you are new to office boxing or Alex is your mentor, take a dive. Buy into his greatness (even if only for survival purposes), and he will want you in his corner to shine the light on his perfection. One way to do this is to offer up a personal flaw that just happens to be one of his strengths. For example, say your Achilles tendon is your footwork, and you are pretty decent with the jab. Alex happens to be great with the jab. Ask him for help with jabs—tell him you know he's very good at it and you're having problems with it. Everyone wins with this strategy: Alex is adored and admired, he gets credit when your jab improves wonderfully, and you get a breather until the next fight.

If you decide to fight Alex, you better knock him out. ***Do not try this if you are a beginner—you will get slaughtered.*** If you are ready to meet Alex in the ring toe to toe, leave him in no doubt about your power or the message packed in your punch. Alex is blind to his shortcomings. Sometimes it takes a lot to get through to him, and reasoning won't work. If you want him to respond, you're going to have to force-feed him with tough love. There are two ways to take care of Alex: a TKO (technical knockout) and a KO (knockout).

For a TKO, you need to get him to realize that some aspect or way he does things needs to be changed—and he must make the change. In a TKO, you don't have to get Alex to admit he made a mistake or isn't perfect. If you get a TKO against Alex, expect him to ask for a rematch.

For a KO, you need to let Alex know (indirectly) that you see him for what he really is and that you can expose him. Don't go for a KO unless the stakes are high and you have enough dirt on Alex to cause a huge crowd reaction. Examples of good dirt include unethical behavior, endangerment of the company's good name or financial status, and being publicly shamed for a mistake. If you KO Alex, he will leave you alone (until he can find a way around your defense).

No matter the outcome of your fight with Alex, don't be surprised if after a round with him, he comes up to you and congratulates you on your jabs or footwork. This is his way of repairing his image. You're supposed to congratulate him back, and then you will both be friends until the next fight.

Ring Tips

- Until you have developed your defense and skills, your best strategy is to stay out of Alex's reach as much as possible. Bulk up so you appear to be capable of flooring him, but avoid actual fights until it's unavoidable.

- Sometimes the safest place to be with Alex is in his corner. Beware of staying in his corner, however, because this strategy isn't all that safe. It's like moving into a clinch with your opponent so he doesn't get enough extension and power behind his punches to hurt you. If you are in Alex's corner or he is your mentor, he may see any imperfection in you as a reflection on him. If you disappoint him, expect to be tossed out of his camp—and possibly into a fixed fight that you're sure to lose and he's sure to benefit from. If Alex is ever in serious danger of failure, perceived or real, all bets are off. He'll offer up the easiest scapegoat—so always keep up your defenses.

- Once Alex knows of your existence in the office, you are in the ring with him. He doesn't waste time or effort sparring in the gym; all his fights are for real.

- Once you get in the ring with Alex, the fight is never over. Be prepared for him to show up in your worst enemy's corner, bribing the officials, or convincing management to strip you of your titles.

- A good percentage of managers, especially the higher in the organization you go, are like Alex. As a matter of fact, they probably hired him and will protect him just because he is like them. If you complain to them about Alex, odds are they will think you are the problem.

Matchups

If Alex is your boss, the easiest strategy is to just move to another gym. However, Alex and his type migrate to upper management like reporters to the winner's circle—so you're bound to meet him, no matter where you go. Your first line of defense is to name your opponent. You'll know it's Alex if he expects you to work unrealistic hours, takes credit for your work while giving you no recognition for it, expects your work to always be sensational, demands your admiration and loyalty (but returns none), uses his power inappropriately, and is generally rude. Also, realize that everything in Alex's life is about him—so don't take things personally; it's not about you. Keep up your training, work on your defense, and watch him for weaknesses in case you have to knock him out.

If Alex is your co-worker, you don't have to worry about being fired directly by him, but you do have to worry that he will work behind the scenes to get you fired. As a co-worker, you may not easily see Alex for what he is. Some of his traits include applying rules one way to himself and another way to everyone else, taking what he wants (even if it's yours), getting you to do his thankless tasks, and being totally insensitive to your needs and feelings. Again, Alex is all about Alex, so don't take things personally. Keep up your training and your defenses, and look for his weaknesses. In particular, get the credit for the work you do, and watch for him to be jealous of you. One more thing: watch and learn from his ability to sell himself to upper management. Alex's skills in this area are finely honed. You'd do well to learn how to use them—and see them for what they are.

If you supervise Alex, it's not any easier than working with him or being managed by him. Actually, it can be more dangerous because you may not peg him as an opponent or may underestimate his fighting skills. As your subordinate, Alex will suck up to you, work to win your approval, and show interest in learning everything you know about making it to the top. If you let this diet of praise go to your head, you probably won't see his knockout punch that follows quickly behind. Alex is on his way up the ranks and sees you as a contender he must fight to continue his rise to fame and fortune. He'll work hard to meet his goals, not yours. He'll flatter you and allow you to mentor him, but only until he feels he's ready to take you on. You get no loyalty from him. As a matter of fact, the odds are he'll rat you out to your boss just for a chance at a promotion (his evidence will probably be fake or exaggerated). So keep your hands (defense) up. Don't ever share your personal business with him. You can play to his ego to influence him to do the work required and even to get him to get along with his peers. Use your jab often to let him know he has to play by your rules.

Fight Commentaries

The Rock versus Golden Boy

Lisa "the Rock" and her co-worker Greg "the Golden Boy" got a new manager. After a few short weeks, they realized their new manager was incompetent. Neither Lisa nor Greg could stomach working for someone who was so obviously beneath them in skill and experience. After complaining to each other about the situation, they came up with a solution: they would go to their old friend Boyd to complain about the new manager, and Boyd would make things right. Their old friend Boyd just happened to be the head of the division and had the power to change the situation.

Lisa and Greg set up the meeting. Once they began discussing the situation, they could tell Boyd was somewhat ill at ease. Greg credited Lisa with the idea and went to a neutral corner for the rest of the discussion. Lisa, who didn't usually get acknowledgement from Greg and hadn't picked up on the significance of Boyd's mood change, took the lead in complaining about the situation. When the bell rang, Greg won by a landslide. From that point forward, Boyd thought of Lisa as a complainer and never took her arguments or side as seriously as Greg's. What happened?

Boyd was ill at ease because he wished Lisa and Greg had gone through regular channels and pushed the complaint up each rung of the ladder instead of jumping immediately to him. Greg realized Boyd was perceiving the visit as a mistake and, in the style of Alex the Great, dished the mistake off to Lisa.

The Apprentice versus the Master

Match: Dave Takes a Dive. David, the Apprentice, interned at a prestigious mental health institution. His supervisor was Jim (the Master), a man well respected in the field of psychology. David was pleased to have Jim as a supervisor: he would learn much, and it would look good on his curriculum vitae when he was done. As the months went by, David's mood changed from excitement to resentment. He worked long hours; none of his work seemed good enough for Jim; and when he did get something right, Jim took the credit for it. To make matters worse, David was falling behind on his routine paperwork—and he knew staff were going to complain to Jim about it.

David set up a meeting with Jim. In the meeting, he told Jim that he was having problems diagnosing patients who presented particular symptoms that could be the result of any number of illnesses. He asked Jim for insight, mentioning he had read the book Jim had written on the topic, but said he wasn't sure he understood the core concepts (and that it was making him fall behind on some other work). Jim was happy to work with David on the problem. Later, when staff complained about David's paperwork, Jim defended David, saying he was going to be a fine doctor and would catch up with his paperwork soon. What happened?

David figured out that Jim was Alexander the Great through and through. He felt he could still get a lot out of the internship as long as he praised Jim regularly and reflected well on him by doing good work. When David started falling behind, however, he knew he had to ask for help and be careful how he did it. He asked Jim for help in an area of David's own strengths: diagnosing people. He knew Jim would be flattered, and he knew the results would be good because it was something David did well. Jim was flattered and helped David. When David was later praised for his ability to diagnose, Jim took the credit for it. Because David was a student who reflected well on himself, Jim defended David on the small issue of paperwork.

Re-Match: The Apprentice Knocks Out the Master. Toward the end of his internship, David began taking credit for his work and tried to get transferred to a different supervisor. This caused clashes with Jim. Then David found out the situation was much worse: Jim was discrediting his work, which would ruin his chances to complete his degree. David met with Jim. He congratulated Jim on his latest book. He asked Jim what he thought would happen if it was discovered that a prominent doctor and author was breaking ethical standards by having an affair with his intern. Jim was quiet. David mused that it would not be good for the author's career. Then he transitioned to discuss his own career and his desire to be transferred to another supervisor so he could experience a different area of mental health. Jim agreed and walked out of the ring. What happened?

David knew Jim was having an affair with one of the interns, which is highly unethical. Because he felt his career was at stake, David used the information like a knockout blow to get Jim to back off. Jim realized that if he didn't leave David alone, he would take a terrible beating in the ring and in the press. He walked away and let David be—this time.

★ ★ ★ FAITH "THE PHANTOM" ★ ★ ★

Alias: The Misfit, Schizoid.

Record: Avoids the ring, preferring to get punches in through others or out of the limelight. When she does fight, it is to the death.

Division: Spoiler in the lower-weight classes.

Reach: Limited.

Height: Lower levels of an organization.

Manager: Fear of annihilation pushes her to be hyper-vigilant about attacks and to create an existence independent of the physical self.

★ ★ ★ ★ ★ ★

Fighter Profile

When you first meet Faith, you may think she is not into office boxing at all, much less a fighter. She's not built like a fighter; she doesn't seem to be in touch with her body and might even seem clumsy. You see her and you think: "She couldn't box her way out of a paper bag."

She doesn't appear to have the mental toughness to fight either—she's often unfocused, spacey, detached. Even she might not feel like she's normal. She may ask you how she should feel, as though she were an actor trying to figure out the motivation for the part she's playing. Keeping her distance in and out of the ring, Faith rarely develops anything more than superficial relationships.

With all these handicaps, Faith can still be a good performer for the company. She identifies closely with her work and achievements. Often the perfectionist (who suffers bouts of procrastination from time to time), Faith is also very accepting and puts up with unfairness, heavy workloads, and changing goals with seemingly great calm. When she's stressed, she's prone to anxiety attacks and paranoia.

Faith tends to work out on a higher plain. She doesn't get sweaty actually working out in the gym or the ring; rather, she intellectualizes the game, like a sports writer. Like most writers and athletes, she has superstitions—except that hers tend to be larger, along the line of phobias. Also like most writers, she has a very rich imagination.

Defense

Faith goes to great lengths to avoid office boxing. She can smell someone stewing for a fight a mile away, and she'll take steps to leave the ring (and the building) or—if it's in her power—shut the fight down. If she's caught off guard and suddenly finds herself in the ring, she may play possum just to avoid the fight.

If you are trying to force a response from Faith, her removed attitude and odd mannerisms may make you feel like she is goading you into a fight. That is not her intention. If she takes on your ideas as her own or projects her moods on you, it isn't an attack. If you draw her into a fight and she can't avoid it, she may call you irrational, out of control, or even crazy.

This fighter has game face in spades. You won't know when she's okay, hurting, or even on the mat. You need to watch closely so you can tell, because if you push Faith too far, she can go berserk.

Offense

The more time you spend around the ring, the more you'll notice that Faith gets her fair share of punches in. As sure as a right punch follows a jab, Faith gets angry, and that anger finds its target. Faith can be a master at passive-aggressive fighting—guerilla fighting—where you can't see your opponent and you rarely know how much damage you've done even when you land a punch.

Faith has another offensive weapon that she rarely uses: the berserk (also known as going postal). If pushed beyond her tolerance level for stress, she is capable of physically taking people out of the game.

Why Are You Fighting?

There are three main reasons for Faith to fight:

1. You attacked her (perceived or real).
2. Payback (passive-aggressive strategy for an old attack that's still fresh in her mind).
3. General revenge when you happen to be in the ring (she's gone postal).

In the Ring

When you're in the ring with Faith, the most important thing is to get a read on which offense she is using. If she's gone berserk, hit the alarm, dive for cover, and save everyone you can. Drop her as quickly as possible if you can safely do so. I'm not kidding.

If she's merely being passive-aggressive, let her know your corrections, etc., are not personal. It's the job, not the person. You still like and will get along with her. Let her know you prefer to work this out quietly without having to go to the ring. Do the least amount of damage necessary if you have to punch, but be honest—don't offer false friendship or praise.

When possible, get third party verification of bouts. Copy someone on the e-mail, have a witness to what was said.

Ring Tips

- Faith takes your criticisms—punches—very seriously. She'll replay the tape over and over in her mind. She goes over the attack again and again, creating different endings, all of which have a disastrous impact on her life. She formulates responses to save herself and revises them over and over again. Her version of your actions will often bear little resemblance to what really happened.

- Each punch you think of throwing, do throw, and land are seen by Faith as attacks. She thinks of each blow as a potential knockout blow. She doesn't understand why this is happening to her. For her, this isn't a game—it's survival.

- Don't push Faith. Hit her when you have to, but don't light into her with a barrage of punches. Hard pressure makes her explode.

Matchups

It would be extremely rare to find Faith in a management position. If Faith is your boss and you manage yourself well, you should do all right. If you know how to effectively manage your boss (see Managing Your Boss article in the resource list), you'll do better. Faith usually manages the way she would like to be managed: hands off. She's so much an isolationist that you're bound to have more problems with the people she doesn't communicate with (such as other departments) than you will have with her. If you do have issues with Faith, your best strategy is to keep it logical. Use emotion and you'll punch yourself out before you see any effect on her. Faith will be a good test of your communication skills. She prefers e-mail to face-to-face conversations and will rarely attend a social function. What will seem to you to be the barest rapport will seem much, much more to her. Remember: Faith is not a people person. Don't take it personally if she doesn't care about your personal goals, make allowances for your family needs, or seems to ignore you. Work on self-management so you don't inadvertently cause her to replay incidents with you, learn to manage your boss (suggest solutions when you present problems, understand what is important from her perspective, and keep her informed of your progress and issues), and keep it logical.

If Faith is your co-worker, you will probably have even less interaction with her. Again, remember that she can only handle a small amount of socializing. If you're in an office environment, you might find she responds better to e-mail than conversation. Faith is a hard worker who is usually technically adept. Avoid taking advantage of her or poking fun at her social ineptness, treat her with quiet respect, and you'll go a long way toward never having to meet her in the ring. In a fight, try to keep from gathering a large crowd of onlookers and keep your offense and defense logical.

If you supervise Faith, micromanage her at your own risk. Pressure will cause her to withdraw—extreme pressure may cause her to explode. Faith doesn't have drive and ambition like other workers, so don't expect her to work hard to earn a raise or move up in the organization. Try to place her in roles that don't require customer contact, play to her strengths, and give quiet praise. Keep records of work tasks and deadlines so there cannot be any question about what was agreed upon. Since Faith's weakest skill is communication, set her on a regular status report schedule and emphasize what information is critical and how it needs to be conveyed. If you have to fight, do it in private, and keep it as calm and logical as you can.

Fight Commentaries

The Press and the Paper Tiger

Joe "Press" runs a small newspaper. One of his employees was Tom "the Paper Tiger," a part-timer averaging twenty hours a week who did small piece work (running errands, etc.). Tom expressed a desire to have more hours. Joe liked Tom: he was on time, conscientious, a bit shy and quirky, but overall an all right guy. So when another employee started having health problems, Joe asked Tom if he'd like to learn some layout and press skills, which would lead to more hours. Tom said he'd have to think about it.

Tom thought and thought and thought about it. He wasn't sure he could do the new work (even though he would get training). He wasn't sure he could handle the stress (a mistake in these areas can cost the business time and money). He wasn't sure he really wanted more hours (he had gotten used to his schedule and had learned to live within his budget). The pay would be the same; he still wouldn't be full-time with benefits; it wasn't really in his field (sociology); and he was comfortable with the work he was doing.

Joe was surprised Tom hadn't jumped on the opportunity. Joe was also wondering how long Tom was going to take to make his decision. And he wondered if Tom was weirder than he had realized and maybe wasn't a good person to have on payroll at all. The guy was so totally into music that he really couldn't talk about cars, sports, or anything else—when you got him to open up at all.

Finally, Joe took Tom aside and said he'd need a response by the next day. Tom was visibly shaken by the meeting and deadline, but he came in the next day and said he could learn the layout skills but not the press work. What happened?

Joe realized that Tom was not like most of his other employees. He gave Tom time to think over the offer and then gave him a deadline when his response took too long. Tom met the deadline. Joe didn't understand why Tom didn't want to learn both new skills but accepted it as another odd quirk in an otherwise good employee. Tom was a little edgy during the training, but once he had a solid grasp on the layout skills, he calmed down to his usual quiet self and continued to be a dependable employee.

Tom's view of what happened was quite different. He was pretty sure that the employee with "health problems" was forced to leave. Tom was worried Joe would be coming after him next. And then Joe demanded he pick up all the work from the guy he fired! And the work was all things Tom had never done before—Joe was definitely setting him up to fail. Somehow Tom learned enough tasks well enough for Joe to let him keep his job.

The Heroine and the Cad

Jane "the Heroine" worked as a line worker on the night shift at a manufacturing plant. Her life was pretty much work, soap operas, and romance novels. Although she didn't have a car, she got rides from female co-workers and rarely missed a shift (she'd call a taxi if no ride was available). During the commute to work, she usually discussed what was going on in the soaps. During breaks she pretty much kept her nose in a book.

Supervisors never had cause to complain about Jane. She could work several different machines, had good output numbers, and always came back from break on time. She wasn't what you'd call a team player, though. She went to the small celebrations if they were at the plant (a birthday, a commendation, a new product line), but she didn't volunteer for any group-type work and didn't socialize with workers once her shift was done.

Jane had been with the company for just over ten years when her supervisor, Jake "the Cad," started having problems with her. Jane started taking more sick time, which she had accumulated plenty of—it was just that it seemed to be growing into an absenteeism problem—and her output numbers were going down. Whenever Jake asked Jane if things were okay, she said everything was fine. He could tell she wasn't comfortable talking to him, so he asked her co-workers about her.

The story he got back was that Jane was a loner who didn't make many friends. If she did make a friend, the relationship was pretty superficial and ended as soon as Jane felt she had been slighted. Throughout the years, she had gradually alienated or shut herself off from most of the other workers and now was having problems finding someone to give her a ride to work.

Jake met with Jane to discuss things. He told her that her output was down and that her absenteeism was getting to be a problem. He told her that he knew about the carpool situation but that there was nothing he could do. He gave her some tough love advice: learn to drive. Jane's work and attendance became more erratic, and then, two weeks later, she disappeared. What happened?

As Jane had more and more trouble getting a ride into work, she began formulating a theory that some of the people at work were out to get her. Because of her growing fear of her co-workers and her lack of reliable transportation, she began using up her sick leave. Her fear led her to decide to move to a different apartment, and she didn't notify her roommate because she was afraid of a confrontation. The confrontation happened anyway when the roommate learned Jane was moving out through a chance encounter with the landlord. Then her boss confronted her at work. Her world was falling apart. On the day she didn't come into work, she woke up, ran to the neighbors, and asked them to call the police because her roommate was hiding in the apartment with a gun and was going to kill her. The police came, questioned her, and took her to the hospital, where she was treated for a psychotic breakdown. The roommate was at work, and there was no gun.

★ ★ ★ KATY "THE CHAOS KID" ★ ★ ★

Alias: The Litigator, Borderline.

Record: Has had her share of losses but loves to fight.

Division: Welterweight, but she takes on fighters in all weight classes.

Reach: Long.

Height: Lower and mid-levels of an organization.

Manager: Fear of abandonment and a chaotic childhood environment forged this boxer, who fights with no concern for the damage she inflicts or takes.

★ ★ ★ ★ ★ ★

Fighter Profile

You may not believe at first that Katy's the cause of the chaos in the office, but keep your eyes and ears open to what's going on inside and outside the ring and you'll see she's in the middle of all the action. She comes on strong and helpful, willing to show you the ropes and even take care of newcomers, and then suddenly her paranoia kicks in, and it's game time: your pal turns pugilist. You can expect her to blame you for all the things that are wrong at work, try to manipulate and control you, change her expectations of your work constantly, falsely accuse you of doing and saying things you didn't, belittle your point of view and self-image, and even physically attack you.

Katy causes a stir wherever she goes. Initially, everyone is talking about the new charismatic "can-do kid." Then, gradually, the crowd splits; half are asking for her to be run out of town while the other half want to give her the keys to the city. Wait long enough and you'll see everyone join forces to strip her of all titles and ranking—and Katy ups the stakes by suing. Some say she has heart to stay in a fight so long. Others see she's self-destructive, to the point she'll blacken her own eyes.

Katy's the girl with the curl in the middle of her forehead: when she is good, she's very good—but when she's bad, she's horrid. When she's good, she achieves near miracles at work, gets along with people, and is one of the best staff the company has ever had. Unfortunately, Katy goes bad at the smallest hint, real or imagined, of rejection. Then she goes into a bout of anger that kicks off into intense, violent, irrational rages—until suddenly she becomes calm and caring once more. She sees things and people as all good or all bad—with sudden switches from one view to the other. No doubt about it; this is the moodiest, most impulsive, and most unpredictable fighter in the ring. Add her quick ability to reverse the situation, place the blame on someone else, change topics, and slip in red herrings, and you see why you need to keep your guard up with this opponent. You ask for her part of the report she was supposed to complete yesterday; she responds that you're criticizing everything she does. You mention you need to review it, and she says you're paranoid. You explain that your manager wants to see it before a board meeting, and she doesn't believe you. And always, always, she demands displays of your trustworthiness.

Katy tends to deny that she needs anything herself and hides her disappointment if her unspoken needs aren't met. But she wants attention and will coddle and mother people as a ploy to get the ultimate mothering she secretly craves. Her coddling can be intensely clingy, and most people in her corner either suffocate or leave. If they leave, Katy goes berserk on them. Expect calls in the middle of the night, lawsuits, and phony orders placed in your name.

Defense

Katy's got so much offense going on in the ring that it's difficult to see her basic defense: pleasing others. She can't be alone—ever. Just the fear of being alone drives her crazy. Her basic move is to look for someone to be in her corner, bring him in and cling hard, realize the person isn't perfect, and then attack him.

Some of her more obvious defenses:

- Take people who don't meet her needs out of action. She'll use whatever methods possible to make you the scapegoat of the office. Expect to not receive party invitations or be included in outings.

- Blame you for the very thing she does. Just when you're about to point out that her personal use of the phone is excessive, she beats you to the punch and accuses you of that very thing.

- Disbelieve your explanations. She'll just flat out say she doesn't believe you. No amount of evidence or logic will change her mind.

Her footwork is phenomenal. Right when you think you have her where you want her, she reverses herself and says of course she agrees with you and always has ... or pushes the blame on someone else ... or changes the subject ... or brings up the one time you did something remotely similar.

Offense

Katy jumps in the ring faster than the referee can sound the bell. Once she starts throwing punches, she comes on fast and furious until you're down. Or until she's down—it really doesn't seem to matter to Katy. She can go through many jobs.

She ducks and slips all your punches. Her trash talk is some of the best. While you're having a hard time connecting on your punches, she lands all her jabs, blaming you for what is going wrong and criticizing your work. Then, when you expect to hear the bell that ends the round, you find she's changed the rules, and you have to endure the agony even longer. Expect constant rule changes, wildly false accusations, and even lawsuits.

Why Are You Fighting?

Usually Katy is fighting you because you've demonstrated you don't need her, or you said no to her. In her mind, that makes you a threat. She may spar with you some if you have something she wants, such as popularity.

You may be fighting because you confronted her or rejected her actions or ideas. If you are in her corner and you show signs of independence or don't stroke her ego enough, expect Katy to react like tabloid news. She'll tell the press box about your indiscretions (real or made-up) and may even go to the powers that be to have you suspended from work.

In the Ring

When Katy is your opponent, it always helps to have support from the crowd and from your corner. These people don't have to be true to you, they just have to be willing to bear witness to reality. In a game of you said / Katy said, the odds are not in your favor (until she builds her record of abuse and deception). Get someone to corroborate your side. Document whatever you can (letters, e-mails, etc.).

Katy moves around a lot. Try to make her stay on topic. Don't allow her to dance through every grievance she has. Also, make her stick to the posted rules as much as you can.

The fight will heat up quickly. Don't react to her rage. (Work on your jump rope skill is handy for this.) Validate her concerns, but don't get into a caretaker position with her. You might hear her pain and acknowledge it's real, but don't offer to help her out or let yourself be taken care of. Sometimes a compliment will help diffuse her fear. Compliment her on something work-related that she does well—never compliment her on something personal, such as her clothing, unless you're willing to risk getting personally involved in her life.

If you're on the ropes and you can't block her punches or get any of your own punches off—and you truly feel you are going down—then you might consider letting her take care of you. Ask her for help in understanding the filing system or how a report needs to be done. This is a worst-case situation because the protection you get in her corner will be short-lived. Sooner or later she will perceive you as a traitor and unleash her hatred on you, until one of you is knocked out.

Ring Tips

- Try to build as much of a case as possible before going to management. If you have weak management, they won't intercede. You should present enough evidence that management has to fire her for breaking essential rules.

- Try to set boundaries. Katy is notorious for accessing other people's work (files, tools, etc.) while guarding hers with multiple locks.

- Keep it professional. Don't get sexually or personally involved with her. If you even tell one little white lie for her, it will come back to haunt you. Also, don't ask anything personal of Katy.

- Just do your work and stay uninvolved:
  - "I'm just here to do my work, so I don't get involved in office politics. I'm not on anyone's side."
  - "I want to finish this up for you on time, so I don't have time to go out to lunch with you."
  - "I want to do a good job, so I can't take your unapproved shortcut to finish up quick."

- Take any praise or blame she dishes out in stride. If Katy loves you today, she'll hate you tomorrow; don't let it go to your head or take it personally.

Matchups

If you work for Katy, you might seriously consider looking for another job. She can do more damage to your career than any of the other opponents listed in this book. On the other hand, if she's on the way out, you might be able to outlast her without taking too much damage. The biggest mistake you can make is to get personally involved, and you're most apt to make this mistake at the beginning of the relationship. Remember your ego's diet, and don't let Katy's compliments go to your head. One last thing: Katy has the energy to go twenty rounds and more. You can't stay out of the ring with her, so choose your battles or you'll use up all your energy the first week.

If Katy is your co-worker, you can bet that she will twist your words, take offense at things you do that are not meant to offend, and claim you are trying to make her look bad. Try to minimize your contact with her, and keep any contact you do have with her at a professional level. Again, the biggest mistake you can make is to get personally involved. She'll jab and yell at you for refusing to bend rules or go out with her—but believe me, those hits and words are nothing compared to the agony she'll put you through if you let her in. When you deal with Katy, you might think of her as a wounded animal. When she attacks, respond with compassion by addressing the underlying wound instead of counterattacking. This will help keep minor issues from escalating into ring events. As always, keep up your guard.

If you supervise Katy and don't set firm boundaries, be prepared for your office to fall into chaos. Initially you can expect good work from her, but that will start to erode as she develops personality problems with people and her work takes a back seat to slug fests. As her supervisor, you must not only find it in you to stay professional, you must also find a way to make her act professionally. Let her know you won't stand for abuse of rules or co-workers. Tell her to come to you immediately if she has any problems with co-workers. When a problem does arise, keep your remarks related to work, remind her that part of her job is working with people who have different personalities, and tell her that you expect her to do her job well. If possible, minimize her contact with other employees. If Katy complains about an employee, you might agree that the other person has some traits that are not perfect, but emphasize that you still expect her to work with that person to get her job done. If you decide Katy must be fired, follow all the rules and document everything. Provide business reasons (did not meet goals) instead of personal reasons (did not get along with other staff). Be sure you don't provide anything for her to use to claim harassment. Katy is notorious for going out with a bang. Get her out as quickly as possible (the overall termination process as well as her last day), get her ID badge, and change the locks.

Fight Commentaries

The Fearsome Foursome Split

Katy, Mingmei, Linda, and Alondra all worked for the same company. Although they worked in different areas, they had become good friends over the years. Linda often taxied Katy around when Katy's car was in the shop (which was often). Mingmei and Alondra pitched in to help Katy with moral support and money when she had a health crisis (which happened a few times a year).

One day Linda was trying to reach Mingmei about a budget issue. Mingmei wasn't returning Linda's e-mail or phone calls. When Linda thought about it, Mingmei had not been eating lunch with them either. Linda asked the others if they had noticed anything or if they knew whether Mingmei was having problems. Katy said she hadn't noticed anything. Alondra said she had noticed Mingmei wasn't eating with them but thought it was because Mingmei was busy with end-of-the-year budget tasks.

Linda stopped by Mingmei's office and got a chilly response to her budget issue: it couldn't be done, and Mingmei didn't have time to explain. That was odd, because Mingmei usually went out of her way to explain the budget to anyone who would listen. Over the next few weeks Linda tried to engage Mingmei in casual conversation, but each time Mingmei treated her like they were strangers.

Alondra soon began to notice that Mingmei wouldn't talk to her either. This made her job much harder since her office worked closely with Mingmei's office. Alondra told the others about the situation, indicating she might have to lodge a complaint with Mingmei's supervisor. The next day Katy took Alondra aside and told her that Mingmei was upset with Linda. Mingmei had found out that Linda told her staff that Mingmei didn't have the education or experience to handle the budget and that she often made mistakes, so staff should always double-check any figures from Mingmei. Katy also told Alondra that as much as this had upset Mingmei, she didn't want to confront Linda—she just wanted to focus on her work, and she would be embarrassed if anyone brought the subject up. Katy said Mingmei might be a bit edgy around Alondra, since Alondra also did budget-related work and might share the same views as Linda.

Alondra and Linda remained good friends, they repaired their relationship with Mingmei, and Katy was eventually fired. What happened?

Several months earlier, Katy needed to get out of town, but Linda wouldn't lend her the car. In retaliation, Katy told Mingmei that Linda thought Mingmei was incompetent. Then Katy sat back to watch Linda deal with having problems in her life! Katy did the same thing to Alondra, because she felt Alondra was always telling her what she should do and how she should act in her personal life. Unfortunately for Katy, the other three women talked to each other, figured out the game Katy was playing, and brought it to the attention of her boss. The boss watched Katy more closely for disruptive behavior and fired her when things got out of hand.

Chaos Thumps Innocence

Joan "of Chaos" and Mary "the Innocent" were secretaries at a university. Joan had been there several years; Mary was new. They worked in the same office and had similar duties, but they worked for different programs and had different supervisors. The first few weeks, they got along well as Joan helped Mary learn the ropes. Mary began to notice that Joan treated students and assistants with disrespect. When those students and assistants warmed up to Mary's friendliness, Joan started bringing in treats and treating them better, actually competing for their attention. Mary let it go. It didn't interfere with work, and the students were getting better treatment.

One day, Mary found that some confidential materials were missing from her desk. She discovered that Joan had taken them and assigned a student to work on them—a clear violation of student confidentiality. When Mary confronted Joan about the issue, she was taken off guard as Joan proceeded to accuse her of the very same thing! Joan did this again: after she accessed Mary's computer for personnel files, she had a computer tech put extra password protection on her own machine—talking so loudly to the tech that Mary could hear her concerns about office staff not respecting privacy. After six months, Mary quit. What happened?

    Mary tried to ignore what she felt were power plays by Joan, the queen of chaos. Mary didn't want to get into fights—she just wanted to do her job. But doing her job became more and more difficult as Joan demanded more attention and crossed more boundaries. When Joan actually slapped Mary, that was it. Mary went to her supervisor and complained. Her supervisor wasn't willing to discipline Joan, so Mary found another position and left.

★ ★ ★ SAM "THE SABOTEUR" ★ ★ ★

Alias: The Backstabber, Passive-Aggressive.

Record: Poor. Wins rounds by making you look bad but rarely wins the match.

Division: Lower- to Middle-Weight class.

Reach: Short.

Height: Lower levels of an organization.

Manager: Deeply rooted ambivalence about himself and others creates this fighter, who excels at making others look bad.

★ ★ ★ ★ ★ ★

Fighter Profile

Sam is the kind of slugger who loves to make you look bad. You throw a boundary-setting jab that glances off him, and he makes it look like you decked him for no reason. You hit him in the body, and he acts like you hit him below the belt. He plays everyone—the crowds as well as you—for sympathy.

His trash talk is all about being misunderstood, unappreciated, and victimized. If you give him a raise, it's not enough. If you give him a reward, it's too late. Ask him to pitch in and help out, and he says you're dumping on him. If Sam hangs around long enough, though, the crowd will see him for what he is and award you the victory. He is the most pessimistic, ill-tempered, spiteful, and malicious opponent you'll meet in the ring.

Sam is "Mr. Doom and Gloom," even when things are going well. He is envious and resentful when others are more fortunate. He acts like he got his lights punched out in his last fight—even though you remember it as just a reminder to get his paperwork in on time. When Sam tries to lighten up, his humor is laced with sarcasm and hurtful jibes.

Sam's bad temper shows in fits of fussiness, arguments, and protests against what he sees as unreasonable demands, which everyone else sees as his everyday responsibilities. If he doesn't want to do something, he will sulk and argue. If he does finally do the work, he'll grumble all the way. He's a guy who becomes enraged over trivial issues and ignores larger problems all together.

Sam often sees red around authority figures. If you're in a position of power, expect to constantly be in the ring with him. Even if you're just a co-worker who happens to get along with your managers, you can expect to be the target of Sam's envy and resentment.

When Sam really doesn't want to do something, he steps it up a notch. The work he just couldn't get to is exactly what others need to complete their work. Or he does the work but in a way that makes it useless. He's deliberately rude. He procrastinates when time is essential, he "forgets" he volunteered to help out, and he works so slowly and inefficiently that you are tempted to do the work yourself. He'll cause conflict between the staff (always covering any trace of his own involvement) and then sit back and watch the fireworks.

Sam is known for his ability to duck a blow and counter with a punishing punch. His passive strategy looks like this:

- Procrastinates about completing essential tasks—especially if someone is depending on him.

- Always finds a way to get around doing what others ask him to do. If he does the work, he works slowly or does a poor job.
- Has a tendency to "forget" obligations he doesn't agree with. He also fails to keep his promises.
- Is habitually late (or early—whatever is the most exasperating for others).
- Is absent (sick, vacation) at exactly the worst time.
- Whines about his problems but never seeks a solution for them.

His aggressive side looks like this:

- Agrees with you and then tells others you're wrong. He may also side with others against you.
- Steals, on occasion.
- Only agrees with you if it's you who are wrong; you don't appreciate him, etc.
- Blames other people for his failures.
- Hoards information and refuses to share in order to undermine other people's work.
- Sets up his own standards of "normal appropriate behavior."
- Assumes others know he is angry but never discusses it. Once he gets upset enough, he puts grievances in writing without discussing it or notifying the person the grievance is against.

Sam's ring presence usually alienates everyone who works with him. Sam can sense the mood shift of the crowd, but he never quite gets that he brought it on himself. He just chalks it up to never getting a break or poor management and hunkers down for the next fight.

Defense

Sam's defense is to play the martyr or victim. As the victim, he seeks support from bystanders—and sometimes even his opponent. His strategy is to not do work he disagrees with in some way, to protect himself with what sound like reasonable excuses, and to get under the skin of his opponent until the opponent blows up. When his opponent blows up, it appears that he's lost his temper and is taking it out on poor Sam, who really couldn't help it that his car stalled on the highway coming into work and so, of course, he couldn't finish the reports that were needed this morning.

Here are some ways Sam gets you to chase him around the ring:

- Hears what he wants to hear, which is not what you said. If you don't have it down in writing, you'll be in a shouting match over who's right.

- Moves so slowly (or quickly) that it exasperates you into telling him to move faster (or slower). But he counters that working differently hurts quality ... and again you're in a shouting match, unless you have hard facts about work time and quality.

- Accidentally loses or destroys work. You can't blame him for power outages that wipe out his computer files, people who steal materials from his truck, or the post office for losing the package in the mail. It's hard to believe that so many bad things happen to Sam.

- Behaves inappropriately but has some justification (he misheard you or thought you were joking), so his behavior comes across as justified and yours as overreaction.

- Complains constantly, to the point you want to gag him—which you can't.

- Can't seem to do anything without forgetting something, so you have to closely review his work, remind him constantly how to do his job, and nag him about deadlines.

When necessary, Sam will apologize and promise to do better or try harder. Don't expect him to follow through, of course—it's only what he says to get off the ropes. If his promise-breaking gets to you and you shift into a rage, then he wins two ways: he gets off the ropes and makes you look like a bully.

If something's gone wrong and you're trying to figure out what happened, expect to see some fancy footwork from Sam. Blame rarely lands on him. He'll step aside and let it land on someone less able to defend himself, directly dish it off to someone else using accusations and blame-shifting, or curry favor with the authority figures he despises until the crisis is past.

Offense

Sam's basic offense is to get you to lose your cool and attack him so he can then play the victim. He has finely honed his skills in this area. His innate ability to figure out your buttons enables him to then push them as he desires. And of course any deadline or agreement you established with him is a ripe candidate for sabotage. He uses passive sabotage skills (being late, working slowly, forgetfulness, evasion, and going behind your back to bitterly complain about you) when he is mildly frustrated. He breaks out his more aggressive skills (temper tantrums, hostile statements, rule-breaking) when the stakes are higher. No matter what he is hitting with, he always tries to cover his actions with victim-like reasoning.

- Something someone else did first pushed him to his action.
- Someone's reaction now indicates that he or she harbored certain feelings then, when Sam did something—so he was justified.
- Someone else has poor work values, or questionable ethics, or personality problems that are negatively impacting him.

Don't mistake his grumbling and complaints as offense—they are actually a way he lets off steam. When he is intimidating others and making them feel guilty, unsure, or uncomfortable, consider those behaviors as jabs that he uses for small-time revenge and to just generally feel better about himself.

In Sam's view of things, thwarting expectations of others is a victory—even if he loses his job over it.

Why Are You Fighting?

With Sam, every day seems like fight time. If you get into a full-blown fight, however, it's probably because:

- He's frustrated.
- He thinks you're interfering with his freedom (example: you won't let him do things his way, or you're making him follow rules).
- You've demanded he follow company standards or meet expectations.
- He's at a point where he feels he has to comply with your demands. He sees compliance as submission and submission as humiliation.

In the Ring

When you're in the ring with Sam, make sure your boxing gloves are laced on tight—and don't forget your mouthpiece and cup—because you are in for an ugly fight. If you keep your cool and use strategy as well as power, you have a very good chance to win the match. If you let Sam get to you, you will take much more damage, but you can still win. To your advantage, a fight with Sam has a dependable flow:

- Sam gets frustrated. He gets your attention through inappropriate action.
- You react to the inappropriate action.
- Sam becomes defensive. First he was frustrated, but now he is angry. He starts to lash out at people and claim he's the victim of your tyranny.
- You take control of the situation, setting boundaries and limits to get Sam to stop lashing out and do his work.
- Sam, forced into the corner by your boundaries and aggressiveness, knows he is a victim. He starts telling everyone how he is suffering at your hands.
- You apologize to him to settle things down.
- Sam has confirmation (the apology) that you were mistreating him.

The trick is to stop the normal flow of events.

- To keep Sam's frustration level down, give him brief, friendly attention regularly. Give him as much freedom as possible while still keeping watch over his work. Reward him when possible.
- When Sam behaves inappropriately, avoid becoming angry, controlling, or judgmental. Keep interactions professional, with a tone of cooperation.
- Learn to read Sam, so when he starts to lash out you will see the blow coming, be able to deflect it, and deflate his anger.
- To take control of the situation, set boundaries. Let him know what is acceptable behavior and what isn't (company policy), what you/he will do and what you/he won't do (job descriptions), and what deadlines must be met. When he does act appropriately (especially in voicing his anger), try to reinforce those actions.
- If Sam starts sabotaging or telling everyone how he is suffering, take him aside (disciplining him in front of everyone reinforces his bad behavior) and set down the boundaries again. If he is really frustrated, you might help him determine the steps needed to complete the task that's bothering him. Keep it professional and unemotional.

- Don't apologize to Sam just to settle things down. If you do end up feeling powerless and angry at Sam, change your methods and try again. Every fighter is unique—you have to craft your strategy to fit them.

In and out of the ring with Sam, keep in mind who he is and accept that. Even if he shows signs of becoming a better employee, keep your dukes up—don't expect him to change, and don't depend on him. A victory against Sam often means minimizing the effect of his negative attitude and getting a half-decent day's work out of him.

Ring Tips

- Set and maintain boundaries. One way to do this is to point out inconsistencies between what he says and what he does. Be careful to maintain your boundaries even if Sam appears to behave better—he is prone to backsliding into old habits.

- Don't assume something is done (or done right) just because Sam tells you it is. Make it a habit to verify instructions with him, review progress toward completion, and check work for quality. Also, check with others to make sure Sam isn't concealing or withholding anything from you. Don't blindly depend on him.

- Put as much as possible in writing. It's best if you have a copy signed or initialed by Sam. Make sure you keep your documentation in a safe place.

- Don't get emotional. Present the facts and discuss how the situation can be improved. If he gets to you (you feel guilty, angry, etc.), remember that is what he is trying to achieve with his often unrealistic accusations. Don't drag up old arguments or issues; it plays to his strengths.

- Try to make sure Sam is well informed about what projects, deadlines, and changes are going on in the office.

- If your defenses are weak, you might consider flattering Sam (tell him you see and appreciate the sacrifices he makes for the company). While this doesn't resolve any issues, it does get him to stop whining for a while. You might ask Sam for ideas for improving things. You'll have to ward off some of his snide remarks, but it will help you establish a rapport with him and help him voice ideas appropriately.

- Because Sam uses passive resistance, whenever he directly disagrees or challenges someone, you should give him positive feedback.

Matchups

It is rare for Sam to rise to a management position. However, if he is your boss, you are probably frustrated beyond words. He procrastinates about completing work (your requests for raises and vacation time in particular). Then when assignments are late, he dumps his work on you and calls it delegation. Unless it looks like he is about to be fired or quit, you should consider finding another job. In the meantime, don't let him affect your career: make sure other people know that you are getting your part of the work done. If Sam complains that you are trying to make him look bad, reply that you are only trying to make yourself look good. Avoid voicing your anger and complaints to Sam, as it tends to make him more defensive. Stay clear of getting emotional. Do be persistent about raises, etc., but in a non-confrontational manner. If you aren't persistent, he will ignore the issue.

If Sam is your co-worker, you have probably heard more complaints than a referee does in his entire career. Avoid agreeing—even by nodding that you hear him—or risk having him use you as an example of "other employees who agree with me" when he takes his complaints to the boss. You might sympathize with Sam's complaints initially, but in time you'll see he is a mediocre employee at best. If you hang out with him, you may be branded the same. If you can't get him out of your office, politely ask him to leave, saying you have to get some work done. Above all, don't do work for him, and don't make excuses for him.

If you supervise Sam, you can either learn to live with his ways, force him to be at least a marginal employee, or fire him. If you let him be as is, his negativity will eventually affect others. Forcing him to meet basic expectations will take some work from you and after a while should show results but will require continuing effort. Firing him will take time (you need a documentation trail and a good case against him) and make your life more miserable in the short run but will be less work in the long run. To avoid hiring someone just like him, check all references and ask former employers if they would hire him again (an honest person will tell you no). Use any initial employee probationary period to assess whether you have a Sam, and to let him go if you do. When giving feedback to Sam on his work, expect him to get defensive and give you a long list of why things didn't turn out better. If he is apologetic and says he will do better, follow up with him to ensure he didn't just throw that comment at you to get you to back off. If he does get to you, don't let him see it. Remember that he dislikes anyone who has power or control over him and is convinced that he is right in his view that you treat him poorly.

Fight Commentaries

Old School versus New School

Ben was an old-school artist who worked for a state agency for twenty-odd years. He had a flex schedule, so he arrived at work an hour before the rest of the staff. He came in, put away his coat, put on the coffee, waited for it to brew, poured a fresh cup, and then called up one of several friends to talk about the weather coming into work, office politics, or something he had seen on TV. After about forty-five minutes he settled down to work. He greeted everyone—including friends—with a growl. People accepted that Ben was an artist and as such was "temperamental." Even the department director was careful around him.

Lucy was a newly hired graphic designer. It took about one hour for the rumor mill to let her know about Ben—and that he was not at all happy that a graphic designer had been hired. Ben believed that electronic art was junk; he didn't know how to use a computer, and he was worried Lucy was going to replace him.

Lucy was good with the computer, but she was no artist. So she had to go to Ben for artwork for the department newsletter. Ben provided her with pieces grudgingly—and usually late. Once, Lucy asked him to draw something specific for an article: a man with an umbrella that shielded him from a downpour of paper. Ben drew a man with an umbrella and a downpour of paper—but instead of the umbrella acting as an aide, it trapped him. Although the artwork met the criteria, it could not be used. By the time Ben retired, he and Lucy were compatible. What happened?

Lucy realized Ben was not leaving his position any time soon and that she would have to find a way to work with him—and get him to work with her. To that end, she complimented his skills and work, let him know that her artistic skills were limited, didn't rat him out to his supervisor for his poor work habits, stayed neutral when others argued about Ben's temperamental side, and occasionally asked him for advice. This strategy gave Ben positive feedback for things he did well and didn't force him into a defensive posture. He never changed his personality, but he did gradually begin to work with Lucy once he realized she wasn't a threat.

Telephone Tag

Rita was hired by a company to help update their call center software. Her team's efforts included documenting the phone menu and adding software so a specific screen, depending on what phone menu options the caller had chosen, would pop up on the call center advocate's computer when they got the call. Tim was company's phone system expert. Management knew him to be a difficult and overbooked employee, so even though he should have been on the team, they didn't assign him to it. Because of his expertise, the team needed to work with him daily. He proved to be a difficult resource for the team. He lost documents, he missed meetings, he had chronic health problems that seemed to flare up at the worst time, he always managed to implement requested changes incorrectly, and he complained that all the problems that came up were the team's fault. Within six months, the project was successfully implemented on time. What happened?

Rita realized that Tim's cooperation was essential to the success of the project. Although he wasn't allowed to be on the team, Rita treated Tim as though he was. He was invited to team outings, he was kept apprised of team tasks and progress, his input was requested on all telephone aspects of the project, and they included him in celebrations. Rita also got his desk, pager, mobile, and home phone numbers. She learned where he liked to hide during the day. She instructed her staff to treat Tim with respect and kid gloves—no matter how upset they were or how wrong they felt Tim was. If anyone had a skirmish with Tim, they were to tell Rita immediately, and she then smoothed things over. She kept copies of all essential documents and any communication between the team and Tim. Tim liked being included in the project. Although he didn't always like being tracked down, he felt important and appreciated. It didn't always work perfectly, but it worked well enough.

★ ★ ★ STELLA "THE BELLE" ★ ★ ★

Alias: Prima Donna, Histrionic.

Record: Lousy, but memorable.

Division: Featherweight.

Reach: Limited.

Height: Lower levels of an organization.

Manager: Early exposure to unresolvable double-bind situations created this fighter, who will do what it takes to be the center of attention and avoid introspection.

★ ★ ★ ★ ★ ★

Fighter Profile

When you think of Stella, you think of the round card girls who are the between-round entertainment. She's pretty, she's sweet, she's sexy—not a threat at all. But this beauty is a fighter, so remember your training: everyone in the office is a potential opponent. Keep your guard up if you don't want any trouble from Stella.

In the office, Stella is usually outgoing and assertive. She enjoys attention and has a knack for getting it. Her flair for the creative aspects of work, her ability to entertain, and her personal presentation make her a crowd favorite. Hang around the gym when she's working out, though, and you'll see a different side of Stella.

There is always a crisis going on in Stella's life, and she shares the drama with anyone who will listen or come to her aid (don't expect her to actually act on good advice, however). Her emotional outbursts are so frequent and distracting that it's hard to get any work done when she's around. While she's great with the ideas, she's worthless when it comes to the details. She's definitely a high-level thinker with no real knack for details.

When Stella doesn't get the attention she feels she deserves, she puts on quite a show to get it. Never mind if her tactics aren't quite ethical or legal. To Stella, the important thing is to keep the spotlight on herself. Her flirting and sexual escapades are legendary, her wardrobe and makeup always make the office buzz, and her exaggerated emotions and theatrics keep people off balance for days at a time. Her nicknames and little jokes can be amusing, but her affected speech, such as baby talk, quickly wears thin.

If work is slow, you can expect to find her in someone's office pouring out her problems, flirting with them, or showering them with compliments. If work is busy and she's not getting the attention she needs, she'll interrupt conversations, play up everyday events as fantastically great or devastatingly poor, or just be rude. If there's something she wants, she'll be as seductive and enticing—or helpless—as possible to get it. When her tactics fail, she shifts into immediate anger and retaliation, having no patience for disappointment or delayed gratification.

Other people in the office see Stella as insubstantial and indecisive. Their view is understandable, since Stella's style is vague and imprecise. Her initial take on a situation is to go with her gut feeling—hunches are more important to her than facts. Because she's so concerned about other people's opinion of her, she tends to change her mind on issues every time she talks to someone new—especially upper management.

You helped her out of a corner once, and now she considers you her best friend. You consider your relationship with your jump rope more emotionally intimate than your relationship with Stella will ever be. Stella comes across so phony and overly dramatic that you swear she belongs on one of those wrestling shows instead of in a boxing ring.

Defense

Stella's defense is pretty basic: diversion. If things are getting uncomfortable for Stella, she will:

- Create a crisis (so the issue is delayed or forgotten).
- Change the subject.
- Have an emotional outburst.
- Close the discussion quickly (prematurely).
- Leave (take the day off or quit).

If she feels someone is not on her side (doesn't "like" her), she may act helpless or flirt to win approval. If necessary, Stella will push her flirting to sexual advances and an affair to get the support she feels she needs. The affairs are usually short-lived.

Stella's skills at detecting other people's reactions to her is amazing. Many people get stuck in her corner because they fall prey to her vitality and sexuality. If you don't get suckered into her corner, her defense will look flimsy to you. Her timing is off, she uses too much or too little power, and she picks the wrong move for the situation.

Offense

Some fighters, including Stella, have limited skills. What works for her on defense, she also uses on offense (and vice versa). If you get confused and don't know if you're fighting or just getting to be very good friends, step back, clear your head, and review Stella's tactics. Her main goal in the ring is not to deck you but to make you like (support, agree with, and take care of) her.

Stella will use diversion, flirtation, and helplessness as offensive as well as defensive weapons. She'll also try to impress, amuse, and flatter people to get her way. She lies if she thinks it will please someone, believing that if pleased, they will like her more.

If her charms don't work, her mood turns suddenly sour. Expect her to be rude, condescending, angry, and even pouty. Her mood may swing back to jubilation or sink to crying, tantrums, and (at worst) suicidal gestures. While all of these seem to indicate Stella is out of control, she is very much in control. She pushes just enough to manipulate you into giving in to her, paying more attention to her, or apologizing for offending her.

Why Are You Fighting?

Since more than anything else Stella wants you to like and take care of her, fights arise when you don't care for her enough. The extension of this is that you don't like her enough to:

- Give her what she wants (attention, projects, days off, etc.).
- Ignore her weaknesses.
- Have an affair with her.
- Help her with her personal crises.

Stella may take your lack of attention as a personal rejection. At that point, she will stop trying to win you over and will instead try to punish you.

In the Ring

First, you need to be sure you are fighting Stella "the Belle" and not Katy "the Chaos Kid." If you ask your opponent a question and don't get a detailed answer—even when you ask for clarification or push for more detail—then you have Stella. Otherwise it's a pretty good bet you have Katy.

Second, remind yourself that even if it feels like you are at the theater being entertained, you are in the ring, and you need to defend yourself. Stella puts on a really good show: she's dramatic, she's attractive (sometimes sexy), and she's intense. Get caught up in the glitter and manipulation of her windmill windup and you'll find yourself nursing a busted nose. You can also expect damage to your reputation just from associating with Stella; at best people will think you're her puppet, at worst her foolish plaything.

Even if Stella pops you a good one, keep in mind that you are a boxer—a thinking fighter—and not someone out to pummel a co-worker into a bloody pulp for the heck of it. Stella has a lot of weaknesses. She can be impressionable, overly trusting, and gullible. Most of the time she is trying to win you over to her fan club, and she only occasionally packs a real punch. All you should need are a few boundary-setting jabs in this fight. Flattening a crowd favorite in the ring could hurt you more than taking a dive.

Take a mature adult stance. Treat her like an adult who must take responsibility for her own actions and life. Don't help her fight her fights, don't get physically involved with her, and don't react to her reactions. If she has a problem, you can be a little sympathetic or recommend where she might get help, but don't take on the role of rescuer in her life. If she comes on to you, politely refuse. If she explodes and makes a scene, cover up to protect yourself and wait until she punches herself out.

Stella knows if you are keeping your eyes on her. She isn't waiting for you to look away so she can pop you a good one, though. She wants you to adore her. She wants your attention and is using it to gauge how she's doing. To keep her happy, always try to keep at least one eye on her —and to make sure she isn't winding up to hit you.

Ring Tips

- Don't rain directly on Stella's parade. If she's totally optimistic, completely in denial, or avoiding something, you'll have better luck if you suggest problems, float other possibilities, and quietly remind her of her responsibilities.

- Be prepared for the crowd to boo you. Stella has done a lot of pre-fight work to get them on her side. She wears sexy gear to please them, she dances and throws some combos to excite them, she's sleeping with the judges, and she's blowing kisses at the people in your corner.

- Don't ignore or withhold your normal care and concern for Stella as a co-worker—even when she is at her worst. If you do, she will detect it and try harder—be more manipulative, flirt more, deliver louder outbursts—to get your attention.

- Stella usually runs at a high level of being overwhelmed. When she's tipping the scales, you can expect more dramatics, outbursts, accusations, and hysterics.

- If Stella takes an absurd position on an issue, using facts to change her mind probably won't work. Your better bet is to suggest that someone she likes has a different viewpoint (which happens to correspond to your view) to get her to shift on a position.

- Always get verification for information Stella provides you. She has a tendency to give people what they want to keep them happy, not minding if that requires stretching the truth or out-and-out lying. She'll also play to your ego (you are such an excellent worker, you do this work so amazingly well …) to keep you placated.

Matchups

Stella doesn't usually rise to the management level, except as a reward for a sales, marketing, or political job well done—that is, an area where pleasing and socializing skills are prized. If Stella is your boss, you may become exhausted trying to keep up with her constant mood swings and doing her work for her. She has great ideas but isn't a good administrator. You get stuck figuring out how to implement her ideas; she takes all the credit. Keep it professional. Do not get personally involved in her life. Her dramatic tirades subside quickly, and she tends to forget the mistakes you make. So don't take her mood swings, positive or negative, seriously. Be patient and tolerant. Stay out of sight when she's in a bad mood. And remember that when the going gets rough, Stella will get going. She'll sulk in a corner, leave for the day, or quit.

If Stella is your co-worker and she doesn't affect your work, you can sit back and enjoy her stories, flirtations, and catastrophes. She tends to be in crisis most of the time, and if you let your guard down at all you can easily get caught up in her life. Once involved, you'll soon find that her problems are endless and it's almost impossible to extricate yourself from her life. Should you have problems in your personal or work life, don't expect her to help you out—her energy is all tied up in her own life. If you spend much time with Stella, your reputation in the office may suffer just by association. Use a gentle jab to politely let her know that you like her well enough, but you have work to do. If you're working together and she's falling behind on her tasks, make a point of giving her approval and more attention when she finishes something. It will help her be more productive.

If you supervise Stella, remember to breathe. Don't let her behavior get to you; stay calm. If you explode on her, it will only lead to a larger explosion on her part. For her, everything is a crisis, and she overreacts every time. When she comes to you with a hard luck story, don't fall for the sucker punch—set your limits, and don't allow her to manipulate you into giving her special attention or favors. Be stern, yet appreciative. Praise her for the tasks she does that are important to you, tell her how much you appreciate her, and stress your wish for her to be productive (so she can keep the job). Since Stella is creative and full of ideas but bad at organization and follow-through, place her in a more creative, flexible role (with good administrative support) if possible, and you will both be better off. People working under Stella tend to burn out, but with a little extra attention and understanding from you, you should be able to minimize turnover.

Fight Commentaries

Snow White and the Dwarves

Mary "Snow White" was the princess of the bureau. She was the secretary for the bureau chief, with other support duties that kept the state office humming. Mostly, though, she was just for show. She was an excellent typist, but she couldn't learn how to use the computer. She didn't like to file. There seemed to always be a crisis going on in her life that required long whispered phone conversations during business hours. She was attractive, dressed very well, and had a ditzy-flirty way about her that made you think it was okay—better even—if you just filed the paper (or typed the letter, or set up the travel arrangements) yourself. That's what the dwarves had learned. Some of them had been working with Mary for over ten years and had learned quite well that a little clerical support work on their part could avoid a loud emotional scene on Mary's part—and that it was well worth it (even though it wasn't in their job description), just to keep things quiet.

The problem came, as it always did, when a new dwarf came along. After a reorganization, Jack became the new bureau chief, bumping former bureau chief Chris to a section chief role. Jack jumped into his work but was soon spending more and more time helping Mary figure out how to set margins in her word processing software, discovering where she had filed the papers he needed, and determining a more flexible schedule for her because of the problems she was having with her teenagers. She also wanted a raise. He thought she was totally incompetent. Within a year Mary got a promotion—and a raise. What happened?

On a particularly frustrating day (Mary hadn't come in and Jack couldn't figure out where she put the file he needed for a meeting), Jack pulled Chris aside and asked him how Mary had gotten and kept her position. Chris explained that in a government agency, it is very difficult to fire a person; it can take years. He also told Jack that Mary was mostly harmless, a good old gal, who did fine as long as she wasn't overly stressed. Jack found out from another dwarf that Chris and Mary used to argue a lot, but after Mary had thrown a huge scene he had given her a promotion, and things had been fine (and quiet) since. Jack also learned that Mary had a heavy flirtation going on with his boss, John. After thinking it through, Jack promoted Mary to a position with more visibility, like attending the many department meetings on organization, etc., but less work. He shifted the work he felt was crucial to the bureau's success to another secretary, began typing his own letters, and became a happy dwarf.

The Countess' Tirades

Eve was a human relations consultant whose basic job was to determine what the client's HR problems were, suggest improvements, and help implement the changes. Her presentations to a client in the Midwest were fabulous. She established a wonderful rapport with management, presented their problems with such wit they laughed with her over their predicament, and then provided solutions that were obviously just what they needed. The longer she stayed, however, the thinner her welcome became, until finally she was asked to leave. What happened?

The client staff assigned to support and learn from Eve quickly grew frustrated. The work assignments she gave them came with only the vaguest direction, and when they brought back the work, she tore it apart, often in front of other team members. She refused to give better direction. She was generally unavailable; she had to attend conferences in other states, work on other projects, and keep her hairdressing appointment (in Baltimore on Wednesdays) because he was the only one who could deal with her sensitive curls.

For reasons never clearly stated, Eve kicked Tony, a fellow consultant, off her team. Tony wasn't sure why, exactly, but it basically ended his career with the company, and he was forced to leave. There were some rumors about Eve and Vince, in administration, just before Thanksgiving. After the rumors died down, Eve demanded that Angela, a fellow consultant, be fired for insubordination, but Angela's manager intervened and, after several days of negotiation, was able to keep Angela. At the Christmas party, Eve got drunk, convinced all the men to be in a picture with her (she was in the middle, laying across their laps), and managed to grope some of them at the same time.

In January the client decided it was time for some consultants to roll off (leave) the project. They picked Eve to go and one of her assistants to stay. Eve was outraged, but the client was firm, and Eve's company agreed. They posted her to a new assignment on the East Coast (closer to Baltimore) and strongly suggested she specialize in the presentation aspect of the job and leave the mundane implementation to a specialized team. She agreed.

★ ★ ★ CONRAD "THE CON MAN" ★ ★ ★

Alias: Antisocial, Con Artist, Sociopath, Bad Boy.

Record: Wins easily but is never satisfied.

Division: Heavyweight.

Reach: Varies according to motivation.

Height: Usually lower levels of an organization, with occasional appearances in mid and upper levels.

Manager: Unknown: possibly an even mix of bad nature and poor nurture.

★ ★ ★ ★ ★ ★

Fighter Profile

Conrad is the fighter who is most willing and able to do what it takes to get what he wants. In that respect, he is a great fighter. But when you feel the brunt of what he will do, come to understand how he is able to do it, or realize what he wants, then respect gives way to fear. And because he is so alien, many people inside and outside the ring become so distressed and confused that they do what is easiest and most natural: they push his strangeness out of mind. They create a reasonable explanation for him and forget what he is really like.

Conrad is goal-driven, but only by his own goal to control and manipulate people through fear and confusion. When he is in the ring, what matters most is beating his opponent. Money, prestige, friendships—they are nice trophies but not as exciting as pulling off the scam. When it comes to achieving his goal, Conrad doesn't care if he throws an illegal punch, is named the winner or loser of the match, or is ejected from the game. Why doesn't he care? Because he has no empathy or compassion—not one ounce of caring for what others feel or think.

Sure, he can get agitated or have an angry burst of temper, and he puts on a good show about caring for the company and others' well-being when needed (or when he's caught doing wrong), but he doesn't really feel a thing. You can't appeal to his sense of what is right; you can't shame him into making amends. You shouldn't expect him to do the honorable thing or to be there for you because you were there for him. If he does anything that regular people do out of a sense of obligation, ethics, sympathy, love, or morals, it is because it gets him to his goal—and only that. When his tactics become boring or don't seem to work, Conrad changes strategies or leaves.

He can be very exciting. He likes to take risks; he likes to get you to take risks. Without empathy, life gets boring quickly. Risk adds flavor. Conrad tells you, "You don't know me, but I already feel we've got a connection. Let's forget about the work deadline for right now and go party, borrow money from petty cash, take a road trip out of town, score some drugs, have sex right here right now. Who cares about tomorrow? Let's live now."

Conrad has ideas and strategies nobody even thought of before. They're a little risky, people might get hurt (but they only have themselves to blame if they do), and the payoff will be tremendous. He talks up his ideas all the time. If something is wrong with one idea, he immediately comes up with another. Although he can really churn out ideas, Conrad doesn't put much into actual work. His own work is incomplete and sloppy. If his work is good, chances are he stole it or got someone else to do it for him.

Some people worship Conrad, some are confused by him, and some don't trust him at all. A person's viewpoint about Conrad depends on which face he is showing them. He's charismatically charming to the "targets" he's drawing into his corner. He flatters them, seduces them, appeals to their kindred spirits.

He's a shifty chameleon to those who've watched him operate. They watch him befriend and betray one person and organization after another. He gets their trust, gets as far as he can on lies and cheating, then vanishes with the money—or gets caught and goes to jail.

He's an icy thug to anyone who gets in his way. He is quick to take offense. He hits below the belt, throws hooks you don't see coming, butts heads, bites ears—anything he feels like.

This is what sociopaths/psychopaths do. Very few are serial killers. Most are so lazy they spend just enough energy to get others to take care of them. Some split their time between committing crimes and serving jail time. The remainder generally move from job to job, as they lie, cheat, and get fired. A small percentage make it to upper management, where they implement risk-taking policies, questionably ethical practices, and some shady deal-making that usually gets the company into fiscal or federal trouble.

Defense

Conrad is an experienced fighter on both defense and offense. He has several effective defensive moves.

- Blend in (pretend to have empathy). Conrad knows he is different, and he knows it would be harder to reach his goals if people realize he has no empathy. By watching others, he's learned to mimic superficial emotions. His fake emotions get him through most situations. The act falls apart when deeper emotions are required or he loses patience or interest.

- Plead for your compassion or pity. Conrad's pity play gets him out of more jams than anything. He appeals to your compassion, asks for one more try, swears he will try to do better, knows he is a changed man, and says he has a plan or new direction to go in. He'll cry real tears, send flowers—whatever will get you off his back.

- Take you into his corner. If you confront him with past wrongs, Conrad will bring you in on his current adventure to make it all up to you. The money, fame, and glory will more than compensate for whatever little thing you think he did.

There are no guarantees, of course, but odds are you'll end up being used and abused by Conrad yet again.

- Assume the role of authority. People generally do what people in authority ask them to do, even if it seems a little odd or possibly unethical. We've been socialized to the point that we rarely stand up, even when we are outraged. Conrad likes to assume an authority role (educated expert, community or business leader, etc.) to give himself the extra advantage. He likes to assume experience that isn't likely to be checked out (likely his own experience in the area is zero or from a book he read).

- Talk fast. Conrad jumps from one idea to the next, making it difficult for others to keep their balance. It is often hard to follow exactly what he is saying; but he's so enthusiastic and the jargon sounds good, so you tend to nod your head and agree. Interrupting him is nearly impossible. If you do manage to point out flaws in his ideas, he will simply change the topic and start down another path.

- Intimidate and blackmail. If you've told Conrad anything confidential, if you've slept with him, or if you care for him, he will use it to bend you to his will.

- Flee. Conrad disappears into the crowds pretty well. He isn't usually pursued, because people are happy just to get rid of him or they're too embarrassed by what happened.

Offense

On offense, Conrad likes to mix things up. He uses a variety of punches, playing with his opponent to see what tactic causes what kind of result.

- Charm and flattery. Conrad is a real charmer. Within five minutes he'll have you excited about meeting him, within fifteen minutes you'll feel he's in your corner—and of course he's the best thing for your ego you've ever had, because he totally understands and supports you. He seduces your mind—and sometimes your body.

- Manipulation. Conrad studies his opponents for weaknesses and uses them to his advantage. All that charm and flattery he just gave you probably led you to confide in or rely on him. Now, if he wants you to do something for him—or maybe just stay silent and not rat him out—he will let you know. Will you do what he asks—or does he tell your boss why you should be fired? Or tell your friends and family that very embarrassing story? Or end your romance?

- Our mild affinity for danger. We kind of like the "bad boy," and Conrad is a natural. He doesn't care what others feel or think, he likes to take risks, and he plays dirty. He'll take the people in his corner on great adrenalin-pumping risky adventures—you only live once! He'll get you to sign off on something slightly questionable—the returns will be great and only a few schmucks will get hurt if they're dumb. You feel like you've got a new, exciting cohort in your corner who is really shaking things up; what you really have is a con man who will string you along until you are no longer useful.

- Lying. Conrad lies as often and easily as he breathes. Usually there's some truth mixed in, but not much.

- Drop his guard. For most fighters, dropping their guard leaves them open to attack. For Conrad, it's different. When he drops his guard and shows people who he really is, they tend to freeze or back away out of fear and shock. What they see is the cold, merciless stare of a predator who thinks nothing more of them than he would of an insect to be crushed if bothersome. In that moment, you fear for your life. Then Conrad puts his game face back on and says something polite. Disoriented, you wonder what happened and can't comprehend it. You either brush it off as a fluke or find a way to stay out of Conrad's path from then on.

Why Are You Fighting?

You will find yourself in the ring with Conrad if you are between him and his goal. You may be a game piece to be manipulated along the way; you may be the goal itself—a person to be defeated. If you are the goal, it is just your bad luck that there is something about you he doesn't like. He will manipulate you or the situation until he has proven to himself that he has won.

Conrad will also pick fights with people if he is bored. He's looking for entertainment, and nothing is more fun than bullying people and getting them to jump to his bidding.

In the Ring

Conrad is a vicious heavyweight fighter with a lot of wins. As soon as the fight is over, however, he is bored again and looking for the next venture. Conrad's need for excitement often gets him in trouble. He scraps his way up to the director level, then gets fired for dipping into petty cash. He runs a tough campaign and gets elected but gets thrown out of office for side deals with developers.

Just like Alex "the Great," Conrad is not the kind of fighter you can "agree to disagree" with. Once they determine you are a threat or target, they will continue to fight with you until one of you is out for the count. You have to decide whether to try for a knockout or take a dive. To get the knockout, you'll have to get Conrad fired.

You won't be able to get Conrad to quit. He doesn't respond to ethical arguments or shaming because he doesn't care. Consequences don't scare him. His reaction to threats is to counterattack—in which case you may find yourself out of a job.

Convincing other people to back you instead of Conrad will be difficult. Most of your co-workers will refuse to join you because Conrad has manipulated them with love or fear. Others will recognize that he is a risk at the work place but think he is worth it for the energy and ideas he brings.

If you decide to take a dive, you'll have to find a way to either make Conrad think he's beaten you or remove yourself from between him and his goal.

Ring Tips

- Realize that Conrad has studied you and knows how to manipulate you. Come clean on anything he could use to blackmail you with. Don't let any of his flattery go to your head.

- Conrad will lull you into a false sense of friendship quickly. Don't let people into your corner until you've known them for a while.

- Don't try to trade punches with him, don't be in his corner, and don't watch his fights. You can't win boxing matches with him because he's willing to escalate it to killing you. If you're in his corner, it's just a matter of time before he manipulates you. If you watch him fight, you'll come to his attention and he'll involve you one way or another. Walk away.

- Be wary of people who show intense interest in you and display "intense" emotions, such as righteousness, indignant posturing, overly patriotic displays, blushing modesty, and weepy sadness. Think of these displays as poor acting. Try to figure out what they hide.

- If Conrad is playing you, you probably feel like you're losing your mind, because nobody else sees it. He's presenting a different side of himself to them; they probably see an upstanding leader of the community. Instead of convincing these people they are being fooled, look for those who see the Conrad you see. Work together to build a case against him.

- Interrupt him; ask for details. This will expose his weaknesses.

- Don't "let it go" or be polite if you get a bad feeling about someone, an authority figure does something he shouldn't, or someone takes advantage of someone else. The longer you ignore his actions, the longer Conrad is disrupting lives.

- Don't forget what you've seen. Don't lull yourself into a false sense of security by thinking you were just imagining or misinterpreting things. When he is acting nice, remind yourself how ugly Conrad has been.

- Don't be a punching bag; don't take repeated abuse from people. A person can make a mistake and hurt you. But if someone makes a habit out of taking advantage of you (three or more incidents), push them as far out of your life as possible.

- Limit the number of "second chances" you give people. Conrad will beg for pity, cry, send you gifts, and swear he'll change his ways. Show him compassion and he's soon back to his old ways. It's understandable that you would give him one second chance, but never should you give him more. Never cover for him or lie for him.

- Sociopaths / psychopaths can't change—and they don't want to change. They see nothing wrong with their lives. They see no problem with how they treat others. You can't change them. If you try, what you are really doing is lowering your guard and helping them achieve their goals.

- Don't give your respect to people out of fear. Fear them; don't idolize them. And remember: it could just as easily be you they are beating up.

Matchups

If Conrad is your boss, you probably feel battered and bruised. He has a short fuse, and you bear the brunt of his anger when things go wrong. He takes credit for all your work and ideas. He works you hard, and when you're about to quit he begs you to stay and promises a promotion (which never comes through). Your best strategy is to quit. If you stay, give Conrad good work, don't break rules for him, and work on a transfer to another manager. If you know there is wrong-doing or cover-ups, gather information you can later use to prove your innocence and his guilt.

    If Conrad is your co-worker, keep to yourself as much as possible. Don't socialize with him, don't share your work with him, and don't do his work for him.

If Conrad breaks any rules, let your manager know. Keep talk on safe topics (sports) and away from work gossip and home. Lock up your possessions.

If you're Conrad's boss, verify his background. Does he really have the education and experience he claims to have? Talk to someone in your human resources department and see if he or she will authorize a criminal record check (and follow through). Take all complaints against Conrad seriously; he is a notorious liar and cheat. Because Conrad likes risk and doesn't care about consequences, you will have to strictly enforce work rules and ethics. He also gets bored easily and can be lazy when it comes to real work, so be on the watch for sloppy and incomplete work. Be ready to fire Conrad if he doesn't perform his job adequately. Because he is such a good manipulator, the decision to fire him may be unpopular—and you may even have to convince your superiors. Once Conrad is gone, you may need a support group for the employees he's harmed.

Fight Commentaries

The Lamb and the Wolf

Jack was an up and coming lawyer. He had a case that was going to make headlines if he could only get all the groundwork done before trial. He met Jill and asked her for a little help. Jill ended up working every spare minute she had for him. He promised to hire her as soon as he could. Months passed, and she started to question what she was doing. Jack told her that when he won, he was going to give her a cut of his share. She mustered up more energy and finished the research. That was two years ago. Yesterday Jill ran into Jack at a campaign fundraiser. Jack, standing with some local powerbrokers, hailed her to his side and introduced her as one of the best researchers he'd ever known—a real asset to any team—someone they should consider hiring on at their law firm. Jill froze. What had happened?

Jill had struggled to complete the work. Every time she was about to quit, Jack praised her or promised paying work or a share of the winnings. He was a great motivator. The day she handed him the completed research, he raped her and then blackmailed her into silence. He went on to win the case and gain a good enough reputation as a litigator to be hired by a prestigious local firm. He never gave her a penny for all her work. He never talked to her until the campaign fundraiser.

She stands there, frozen. Isn't this the guy she hates, now paying her huge compliments and suggesting his firm hire her? She should denounce him, or spit on him, or slap him. But they are in a social situation, and he is being nice. Kind, even. They are in a business situation, actually. There is a possibility this could lead to a job interview. These powerbrokers believe in Jack. Does she expose him? Walk away? Shake hands and smile?

The Fox in the Hen House

Dana was the outcast in the orchestra. She was painfully shy and played the clarinet. Then Stacey came along and befriended Dana. Stacey was rough around the edges, but Dana knew that underneath it all Stacey was vulnerable and needed a true friend. So Dana smoothed things over when Stacey laughed when nice people got hurt, made tasteless jokes, and showed no remorse for hacking into Lynn's e-mail account and sending rude e-mails to all her friends as a joke. Then Dana's parents forbade the friendship and made Dana change schools. What happened?

Stacey didn't actually have the talent she should have needed to play at the college level. What she did have was the charisma to win people over and a well-connected, wealthy family. If she couldn't charm her way out of a situation, her family would buy her way out. When she misdirected freshmen about where the practice rooms were, the teachers admonished her but didn't give her actual warnings. Stacey's affair with the business professor was quiet but talked about. Everyone knew she cheated on just about every test she took, and sometimes a teacher would fail her. She took out her jealousy over Brian's success (he got clarinet first chair) on his equipment. Before the holiday show, she broke every clarinet reed he had. And she started blackmailing Dana for money, even though Stacey had plenty of her own. Dana knew if she was a solid friend, Stacey would heal and learn to trust and stop acting out. Dana knew if she let Stacey down, Stacey would never get a chance to get over the awful childhood Stacey had confided to her. Dana's parents and the school counselor knew better. They knew Stacey's track record; they knew it would never change. The best course of action was to remove Dana and hope someday she would understand.

★ ★ ★ MARK "THE MACHINE" ★ ★ ★

Alias: Perfectionist, Obsessive-Compulsive.

Record: Good in a fair fight.

Division: Lightweight.

Reach: Average (as far as the rules allow).

Height: Lower to upper management.

Manager: Fear of being punished for breaking a rule or being less than perfect formed this tightly controlled combatant.

★ ★ ★ ★ ★ ★

Fighter Profile

Mark is totally committed to work. He's the "all work and no play" guy. His emotions are like his work ethic: very controlled. You imagine that when he fights, Mark takes some classic stance, asks if you follow the Marquis of Queensberry Rules, and then critiques your form while you're trying to hit him.

Like a machine, Mark puts in long hours without breaks, works the details to death, and has flawless output. He has no problem putting his work before his home life. He follows the rules, literally and virtuously, regardless of circumstances. He obeys the people above him and rules the people below him. Mark expects this same effort from everyone else. He's the know-it-all in the gym who puts in the most effort but just doesn't have what it takes to be a contender.

Mark is a perfectionist. His standards are so high that he himself rarely meets them. Still, he pushes himself—and you—to attain his unrealistic goals. He criticizes himself—and especially you—when the goals aren't met. He takes his responsibilities seriously and tries to be the best at each task, no matter how important or trivial it is.

Mark's attention to detail is amazing and frustrating. He has a place for each and every thing, a rule for every occasion, and a system for every task. His way is best, and he doesn't let up on you until you do things his way. Mark doesn't trust anyone else to do a good job. He will take jab after jab after jab at your work until a decent effort looks fatally flawed. You may even find that he's actually redone your work the "correct" way. Getting Mark to skip steps or try something new (such as your idea) is just about impossible.

He's so detail-oriented that it can be difficult to get him to see the big picture. He'll be so focused on something like getting the layout or wording perfect that he forgets it's just an internal draft. Because he can't just slap something together, he's always under deadline pressure. Because he doesn't think anyone will do as good a job as he does, he won't delegate work. He works himself into such a frenzy that he often gets sick and has to take a few days off after a deadline to recuperate.

The mood in his corner is a sterilized cold. There are no jokes, no schmoozing. Everything is discipline, order, reliability, loyalty, integrity, and perseverance. Ask for some understanding, and you'll get an intellectualized assessment of the issue.

Defense

Mark's main defense is the posted rules. Because of that and his loyalty to management, he gets some protection from the establishment.

Mark's secondary defense is footwork. He shifts around so much that you can't connect on your punches. Instead of dealing with the issue at hand, Mark usually shifts to one of three places:

- To the periphery. He will focus on an unrelated minor detail, with a resulting decision on the detail but not the issue.

- To the abstract. He will focus on a related abstract idea and talk it to death, making no decision on anything.

- Between extremes. He will shift between extreme stances on the issue and either won't decide or will make an impulsive decision.

An aspect of Mark's defense that makes him a tough, frustrating opponent to face is that he rigidly controls his emotion. He won't lose his temper, become enraged, and make a mistake in the ring. In fact, the angrier he gets, the calmer he may appear.

Offense

If you ask Mark, he'll say he's never stepped in the ring. If you ask the people who've worked with him, they'll show you cuts and bruises he's recently dished out. Mark swears he's merely following orders, enforcing the rules, and getting things done the right way. Regardless of Mark's explanation of his behavior, co-workers and subordinates around him get beat up.

First, he'll come at you with a "better way" to complete a task. If you don't fall in line, you can expect him to be passive-aggressive (like Sam the Saboteur but much more controlled and low key). He may take on an air of moral superiority and shame you into compliance by picking your work apart in front of others. Sometimes Mark will actually present his version of your work—which you can count on to be flawless—to your boss. And, of course, you can depend on him to use standards, rules, and regulations against you.

Why Are You Fighting?

You are fighting with Mark because you are not perfect. Perfection, of course, is defined by Mark. He expects you to know how things are done and to do them right. Mistakes are not tolerated—no matter how small they may be.

In the Ring

Whenever you are around Mark, remind yourself that he's a perfectionist and he doesn't like to be wrong. That way, you won't be completely surprised when he comes after you for some seemingly trivial thing.

The best way to avoid a fight is to just do things his way. However, if you're set on doing things your way, you might tell Mark that he inspired your idea. This may create an opening for him to consider the idea. If this doesn't work, your best move is to go to his supervisor and argue your point there. If you do go to Mark's supervisor and he agrees with you, in whole or in part, ask him to play the referee in giving the results to Mark and the office. His influence will help smooth post-fight animosity.

When you're in the middle of a fight and Mark is slipping and ducking your punches, use logic and structure to get him to stand still.

- If he's jumping to the larger picture, go there with him. But once the overall need is established, draw him down to the level of detail where the issue is. Show how the resolution of the smaller issue improves the big picture.

- If he's clutching to unrelated detail, try to move him to the larger picture. Once there, draw him down to the detail in question.

- If he's vacillating between high level and detail, try to get all the high-level thinking covered before shifting to detail. If he jumps before you're ready, pull him back by explaining that you don't quite get it, or say that you need to cover one more thing before going to the details.

A fact-based offense is your best bet. Mark's weakness is his anxiety over making mistakes. If you can show that your method will lead to fewer mistakes or less risk, you may lure him into listening to you.

Don't expect to get a final resolution. That would require Mark to feel comfortable with and be absolutely clear on each and every detail. Settle for enough resolution to continue to the next step. Agreeing to disagree is rarely acceptable to Mark.

Read up on Sam the Saboteur; if Mark starts being passive-aggressive, you'll know how to react. Mark's passive-aggressiveness will be harder to detect because he's much better at hiding his anger than Sam is.

Ring Tips

- Mark almost always has a moral righteousness or dogmatic view on life. Avoid discussing religion and politics with him. If your views don't exactly match his, he will find ways to punish you if you don't accept his beliefs.

- Be a gracious winner in any fight you have with Mark. He has been known to occasionally carry a grudge and use rules and regulations to get revenge. While you may win this argument, you may lose your vacation.

- Mark doesn't see how his actions hurt other people, and he doesn't care what others think about him. Don't take any of his jabs personally because he truly doesn't deliver them with anything other than "following the rules" in mind.

- You can build a small degree of rapport with Mark by recognizing him as an expert in his area. When you have time, ask him to explain a company policy. If you have a disagreement, ask him to explain his logic or the rules he's using. You might ask what, exactly, you did wrong and how you can do it better next time. Remember: no matter how well you get along with Mark, he will not bend or break a rule for you.

- Mark tends to agree or disagree wholeheartedly. He's been known to take up the opposing view as fervently as he initially opposed it.

- If Mark has a routine, don't ever mess with it. Although it's tempting to mess with Mark, it won't work because he doesn't have much of a sense of humor. You're liable to cause more harm than fun.

Matchups

Mark is a very demanding boss. He expects a lot and gives little in return. Your only comfort is that he's just as hard on himself as he is on you. Don't waste any effort trying to schmooze him—you're better off keeping to the business and facts at hand. Mark won't do a favor for you because he likes you or even if you have all your work done. You'll get whatever company policy says you're to get. Give Mark a solid day's work, with occasional overtime. Don't ever give less; don't let him know you think eight hours is enough. When he's piling work on you, make him prioritize the tasks and make him aware that the lower-priority items may not get done. When you make mistakes, bring it to his attention immediately, preferably with potential solutions. Mark will criticize you when you fail and will fail to praise you when you succeed. Stay as positive as you can—you're a team player doing your best. On a regular basis (when you can do it sincerely), compliment him on something he does well or thank him for help he's given you. Learn what you can from Mark (efficiency, rules, etc.).

With Mark as a co-worker, you can expect constant detailed criticism of your work. Don't take the critiques personally. Use the feedback if you can, thank him for his insight and say you'll consider it, or let him know (politely) to back off. If Mark's competitive, he'll tell others about your mistakes. If that happens, repair the damage with the others and promote the team concept. (We're a team, we play to everyone's strengths, we work together, etc.) You can help Mark by getting him to focus on his priorities and deadlines. Make sure Mark's obsessions don't keep you from completing your own work. Let him know that some things aren't up for debate, different styles are okay, and you won't try to change him if he won't try to change you.

If you're Mark's boss, you know he's a devoted worker, but you wish you didn't need to supervise him so closely. Set clear expectations and boundaries regarding behavior that will not be tolerated, such as competitive behavior, criticizing others or re-doing their work, and missing deadlines. Help Mark out by giving him smaller, prioritized tasks. If you give him a project, give him a methodology to follow, and ask for regular progress reports. When giving feedback, downplay his need to make things perfect, indicate areas where he can improve, and praise his good habits. Monitor his work more closely when he puts in long hours (odds are the work he's doing is nit picking and not adding value). If possible, keep him in positions where the work is structured rather than vague, and the line of command is clear. Mark is very good at rational, detailed, and disciplined thinking.

Fight Commentaries

The Rules Hit the Road

Rob "Rules" was an engineer at a construction firm; you could count on him to wear jeans and a polo shirt every day. He also brought the same lunch year in and year out. Rhonda "the Road" was the project's no-nonsense clerical support staff who kept the phone call and paperwork traffic flowing smoothly. Rhonda appreciated Rob's professionalism. While Rob was a bit demanding about receiving paperwork on time (down to the minute), he was well organized and could tell you exactly how things were to be done, usually citing the precise page, paragraph, and line of code or contract.

One day, Rhonda started getting complaints that people were receiving two copies of her daily project schedule and issues. Wasn't one enough? Rhonda investigated the situation and found that Rob was sending it out a second time—with specific comments to each person on what he thought they should pay attention to. After some discussion, Rob stopped sending his update. What happened?

Rhonda explained to Rob that the second mailing wasn't necessary and that people were complaining. Rob didn't care because he knew his comments were essential. Rhonda finally told Rob that if he wouldn't stop, then she would—and he would be responsible for keeping staff up to date every day on project and company news. She also told Rob that she had some other tasks he could do permanently from now on. In a huff, Rob stopped his e-mails. Instead, he printed out the update, wrote comments on it, and delivered his insights in person throughout the day.

Principals of Growth

Andy "All the Facts" was a very thorough architect. He did excellent work. Peter, the principal partner of the firm, admired Andy's work ethic. He began to worry about Andy, though, as time went by and Andy didn't move up in the organization. Peter looked into the situation and found that even though Andy had drafted hundreds of buildings and knew the standard building specs by heart, he took the time to research each and every specification each time they came up in a project. Also, instead of using a similar completed project as a starting point, Andy drafted each project from scratch. In Peter's mind, the long hours Andy was putting in were not adding value. In addition, Andy's work was not creative. Andy was not "growing" as an architect. Peter tried to break what he considered to be Andy's bad habits. After several months he fired Andy. What happened?

When Peter gave Andy more advanced work, to take him away from the detail work that was consuming him, the result was that Andy put in longer hours to get the detail and the advanced work done. Peter felt he couldn't justify paying a licensed architect to do apprentice-level work. He let Andy go, with a referral to a shop that would be a better fit for Andy's abilities.

★ ★ ★ NORA "THE NEEDY GNAT" ★ ★ ★

Alias: Clingy, Yes Man, Dependent.

Record: Always loses (because winning is losing, and losing is winning).

Division: The lowest weight classes.

Reach: Limited.

Height: Lower levels of an organization.

Manager: Fear of abandonment and disapproval drives her to please others at all costs.

★ ★ ★ ★ ★ ★

Fighter Profile

Nora is not much of a fighter. She can't decide if she wants cream or sugar in her coffee without someone's input, so it's not often you see her in the ring. If she does get into a disagreement, she'll be apologizing about it for weeks. She seems to be the most gentle, yielding, sweet person you've ever met. Then you get frustrated with her because she never takes initiative, never volunteers a new idea, never does anything without first checking to make sure it is okay, and is always worried she is not doing enough or doing it well enough.

Nora is the reason you go over new policies and procedures again and again. She needs continual training and reassurance from her boss and co-workers to perform her job satisfactorily. Having everyone's approval is extremely important to her. She's willing to do almost anything—even taking a few punches—to get that approval.

She's very unsure of herself. You see it in how she always looks to others for direction, guidance, and feedback. It's a complex world, and Nora feels she doesn't have the ability to deal with it. She puts little faith in her abilities. She'll take the smallest piece of constructive criticism and beat herself up with it as proof of her unworthiness.

To survive in this complex world, Nora seeks protectors. A protector is her champion. She'll do her protector's work, watch his back, take the blame for a situation—anything to stay in his good graces. She not only tolerates mistreatment but goes back for second helpings if she thinks it will keep her safe. While you might think she's given her heart and soul to her protector, if she loses him she will find another one immediately. She fills vacancies faster than a promoter fills event slots.

Nora isn't a good judge of people. She often idealizes them, refusing to see anything bad or imperfect. Because of this and her need to have a protector, you may find her in the corner of some pretty unsavory fighters. In a way, she's a perfect match for rude, unpredictable, paranoid, narcissistic people. She gives them what they want (unquestioning loyalty, help of any kind) as long as they give her what she needs: someone to rule her world.

If you have to rely on Nora to back you up in front of others and you aren't her protector, you will be disappointed. She will take a dive as soon as the first punch is thrown. As soon as someone disagrees or makes an alternative suggestion, Nora agrees with them. When you press her to agree with you, she makes some mealy-mouthed comment about everyone having such good ideas and says that she just wants everyone to get along. When you try to talk to her afterwards about leaving you high and dry, she starts crying and berating herself until you finally calm her down and tell her she didn't do anything wrong. You learn that you just can't count on her in a bind.

Defense

Nora avoids conflict as much as possible. If she finds herself in the ring, she'll either start beating herself up with endless self-criticism or will try to gloss over the whole thing with comments like "It really isn't that bad" and "Of course you're right, because you know so much more than I do."

She cannot stand to be the center of negative attention. To protect herself she may:

- Agree mindlessly with her opponent.
- Yield her individuality and support her opponent instead of get angry at her opponent.
- Offer to do a favor for her opponent in order to right the wrong.
- Become so emotionally hurt that you fear you'll have to call in medical help.
- Cling and submit to her opponent, trying to get him to now protect her.
- Procrastinate to avoid confrontation.
- Deny anything is wrong—or insist that being wrong isn't so bad.
- Become syrupy sweet to her opponent.

Offense

Nora depends on her protector—after all, that is what he is for. If her protector steps in, she will support him. You don't have to worry that Nora will start a fight and then go running to her protector, because truly she doesn't like conflict. If she finds herself in the ring and her protector is not available, she will attach herself to the nearest person (or people) she can find.

Why Are You Fighting?

You will most likely get into the ring with Nora because you have lost patience with her. You've been through the same issue time after time, and all you really want is for her to own up to her mistake, take the initiative to ensure it won't happen again, and just be professional about it.

It's also possible that when you did lose your patience with her, she was shaken by it, and she went to her protector, who is now standing in your office door wanting to know why you had to stir things up. Now Nora is sobbing in his office, and he doesn't have time to deal with all this.

If you are Nora's protector, you could be fighting because you're tired of her neediness and you're trying to create distance from her.

In the Ring

The first thing you should do when you are in the ring with Nora is to remember who her protector is. If you don't want to deal with that person, find a way to end the fight as quickly and calmly as possible.

Your second move should be to end the fight as quickly and calmly as possible. Why do this for such a lightweight fighter? Because if you insist on fighting, she'll recruit a protector (maybe even you, which you really don't want to happen). If there are any witnesses, they will view you as a bully (as Nora crumples to the floor before you even jab at her), and, honestly, you can't convince her to change how she does something in a fight atmosphere.

Ring Tips

- Anything you say to Nora will find its way to her protector.
- Nora tends to do what authority figures tell her to do. Try to get authority figures in your corner.
- Nora is anxious and insecure. Nothing you say or do will change that—even if you become her protector.
- She constantly seeks reassurance. She agrees with people and does favors for them to get them to like her.
- She views everyone but herself as competent.
- Nora relies on her feelings more than her problem-solving abilities. She avoids negative feelings, preferring to make up a better version of reality.
- In or out of the ring, if she considers her relationship with you to be more stable than the one she has with her protector, she will likely try to get you to protect her.

- If you become her protector, expect her to use cajolery, bribery, self-censure, promises to change (rarely kept), and even threats to keep the relationship going.

Matchups

It is pretty rare for Nora to be in a supervisory or trainer position. However, if she supervises you, you can expect she will praise your efforts and give you a steady supply of compliments. While she might tell another supervisor that you do your work well, she would never go out on a limb to protect or recommend you. You may wonder if she knows what she's doing because she constantly second-guesses herself and worries about messing things up. Nora will probably give you tasks and then treat you like the expert. (Avoid becoming her protector.) She presents an unrealistically positive view of the world, so don't count on a raise she says is coming until you have the money in your hands.

If Nora is your co-worker, she may come to you for advice and reassurance. Sometimes she will stop by just to talk because she doesn't like to be alone. Try to walk the line between being nice and becoming involved. Keep things light. She can be a hard worker, but she is not usually creative, doesn't like change, and doesn't want to take the lead (or responsibility) for anything. If you check her work, be careful when you give her feedback; she doesn't take any kind of criticism well.

If you supervise Nora, her oversensitivity and need for constant reassurance probably drives you crazy. She continually puts you in a position of taking care of her: explaining the rules one more time, going over new policy with her in detail, helping her prioritize her tasks, etc. If you feel you are her parent, you are her protector. If you don't mind the role, the benefits are that she will do what you ask, give extra effort, and be calmer. If she has another protector at work, be aware that she will do things for that person even if doing so interferes with her job, which could impact you. Nora is easily devastated by critical feedback, so when you must ask her to improve, don't forget to assure her that she performs well in many areas and still has a job. Because she is unsure of herself, she generally prefers closer supervision or to have her work checked by another. Nora does not work well alone, and she does not like to work alone.

Fight Commentaries

The Shepherd and the Chicken

Deb "the Shepherd" tried to be a good manager, but Sylvia "the Chicken" really pushed her limits. After a year of explaining to Sylvia again and again how to handle client correspondence, pulling "ready to mail" reports and recompiling them herself because a last-minute check indicated Sylvia had once again messed up the order (photos always go in Appendix B, not in the chapters), and having to scrounge around for pens and rubber bands because Sylvia forgot to order those basic office items yet again—after all this, Deb decided she could not teach Sylvia. Even though Deb's other employees had quickly learned from Deb, Sylvia struggled. It must be a communication issue, Deb thought. Not one to give up, Deb decided to send Sylvia to training. And then Sylvia, aged thirty-five, disappeared. What happened?

    Deb found a three-day workshop in Cincinnati that sounded perfect for Sylvia. They discussed it together, and Sylvia agreed it sounded like it would be helpful. Deb shifted her budget around to locate the money for the training, airfare, hotel, and per diem. The day before Sylvia was to fly out, she indicated that her boyfriend was not happy she was going to be gone for so long. Deb talked to her, and they agreed the boyfriend's objection was silly. The day Sylvia was to leave, Deb got a phone call from Sylvia's mother: Sylvia was sick and would not be able to go to work there or anywhere else today. The mother also asked if Sylvia's paycheck could be mailed to her home. Sylvia never came back to work.

    For her part, Sylvia liked working for Deb. Deb was reassuring and helpful. But the idea of going to training—and the way Deb talked about it—made Sylvia fear she would be expected to be perfect and not require any help afterwards. That didn't sound good at all. And if she went to the training she wouldn't be home to help her mother out. Sylvia didn't have a boyfriend; it was her mother's idea to make one up as an excuse. Her mother was busy with her own work and friends and needed Sylvia to keep the house in order and do the shopping. Sylvia was interested in the workshop, but her mother said no.

The Minister and the Forgetful Saint

Trent got along with everybody. He never argued, never took sides, always had a story to tell, and would bring treats to work. James, his supervisor, thought Trent would be a great employee if he could just control his anxiety and remember to do his work right. James had given Trent a materials checklist for loading his vehicle, but Trent always forgot something he needed for a service call. James had given

Trent hands-on training for servicing their product and provided a maintenance cheat sheet, but after six months on the job Trent still messed up basic repairs. There didn't seem to be anything Trent could do without having someone hold his hand. James changed Trent's schedule, and Trent resigned a few weeks later. What happened?

James found that Trent performed best on a crew with an experienced crew chief. Unfortunately, the company didn't have much work for crews. Most of their work was handled by individuals going out on their own. James told Trent that if he couldn't improve his performance on individual work, he would only be able to use him in a crew when there was work. Trent tried to improve, but he didn't. James cut back Trent's hours. Trent left the company because he wasn't working enough hours to make a living.

★ ★ ★ GIL "THE NICE GUY" ★ ★ ★

Alias: Timid, Avoidant, Self-defeating.

Record: Rarely, if ever, wins. Defeats himself before even entering the ring.

Division: Featherweight.

Reach: Extremely limited.

Height: Lower levels of an organization, or a skill specialty position.

Manager: Intense fear of criticism has kept him socially isolated.

★ ★ ★ ★ ★ ★

Fighter Profile

When it comes to boxing, Gill has the least fighting skill. He's no good at defending himself, and his idea of offense is to give his opponent something he baked himself. Gill is perpetually worried about making mistakes and being inadequate, so whether you throw a punch or a compliment at him, internally he twists it to hurt himself just a little bit more. Because he is so sure he is the one at fault, instead of defending himself by blocking or counterpunching, he tries to fix his faults by working harder for—or being even nicer to—the person attacking him.

Gill is the shy guy who quietly cranks the work out, day in and day out. He's afraid to ask for anything (new equipment, a day off, etc.) because no matter how reasonable the request or the manager, Gill's pretty sure things will escalate and he'll be fired over it. He wouldn't dare ask for a raise! Instead, he waits for his manager to notice his good work effort and reward him for it.

If a process changes or Gill is asked to do a new task, he worries that he will mess it up. But once he gets past his fear and does the job, he does it well. He can be very skilled at what he does, but he never believes it.

There's a negative soundtrack playing in Gill's head. Give him a new, faster computer—it must be because he's too slow. Give him a better office—it's one more step toward moving him out of the company. Give him a hefty raise—that must mean you're going to give him new job responsibilities that he will fail at, and then you'll fire him.

Even though Gill tries to be liked, his fears keep him locked inside himself, so he doesn't make a lot of friends. And if you do get to know him, it's hard to spend a lot of time around someone who is constantly picking on himself. It's hard to even give him a compliment.

Defense

When attacked, Gil believes it is because of his own shortcomings. What is his defensive reaction? Cookies and kindness. He'll bring cookies to make up for his mistakes. He'll be even nicer to his attacker to make up for things and hope to win his way back into the attacker's good graces.

During an attack, Gil will be silent and then quietly disappear back to his cube. He will probably come around later to ask the attacker to repeat what was wrong, and then Gil will work hard to fix the error.

He is constantly monitoring his actions and other people's reactions for signs that he has done something that is unacceptable. At the same time, he is continuously criticizing himself over minor and imagined flaws.

Offense

When he's going after himself, Gil's stamina, ring talk, and jabs are amazing. He's relentless when beating up on himself. Point him toward another opponent and it all disappears; he's back in the kitchen baking cookies.

Why Are You Fighting?

If Gil is attacking you (bringing you lots of baked goods and doing you favors), you'll have to figure out what you did that set him to baking. Directly asking him won't work because everything is his fault in his mind. Ask someone in his corner; they might know.

In the Ring

Gil is trying to get you to like him. However, if you eat all the cookies, you will only gain weight; Gil will wrongly think his strategy is working, and the next time you two have an issue, it's back to baked goods and more weight gain.

Here's an alternate strategy. Eat one cookie, and share the rest with the other office workers. Make sure everyone—especially Gil—hears how much you like the cookie and what a good guy you think Gil is. Don't try to make amends with Gil, and don't give him too many compliments—it just won't work.

Ring Tips

- Thank Gil for whatever he gives you as a peace offering.
- If you find out what you did to provoke him, don't make amends directly to him. He will refuse to accept that you did anything wrong or he did anything right. Instead, make amends to the group as a whole, and ensure Gil hears it. Here's a staff meeting example: "Last week when I said I had some new ideas for optimizing resources, I forgot to say how much input I had from everyone, especially Gil …"
- No matter how easy it is to outbox Gil, remember that he is a solid worker you really don't want to lose.

Matchups

If Gil is your boss, you may be frustrated by his constant self-belittling and tendency to procrastinate; while at the same time you are amazed at his skill with everything but people. He gives you positive feedback no matter what you do, which is okay unless you are a hard worker and realize everyone gets the same treatment—except for jerks, who are treated even better! You can't fight his fights for him, but you might let higher ups know when someone is beating up on Gil.

If Gil is your co-worker, you admire his ability to get things done, even if he does barely meet deadlines sometimes. He's a quiet team player. He brings you peace offerings every time you do something that pisses him off; then you give him a small peace offering, and things are back to normal.

If you're Gil's boss, you're happy to have a solid worker who doesn't require much of your attention. It's impossible to keep Gil happy, since he never tells you what he wants and he sees the usual rewards—raises, praise, promotions—as negatives. So you do what you can, and that is generally good enough.

Fight Commentaries

The Orchid, the Mealy Bug, and Pest Control

Wanda had worked for the software company for years when the firm hired Conroy, an up-and-coming star, to manage the user support section where she worked. It took her awhile to warm up to him, but when he confided his fears to her and depended on her more and more, she couldn't help but like him. He understood her more than anyone else at work. She gladly put in extra hours, off the clock, to help him succeed. Sometimes he took credit for her ideas and work, and that made her a little mad, but she never would have told anyone about those process improvements anyway, and they had needed some tweaking (which Conroy did) to be really good. Anyway, she didn't want to be someone who told others how to do their work better. She was glad Conroy took her silly ideas and made something of them for himself; she baked him his favorite peach pie to show him she was okay with everything. He actually got a promotion! But then something went wrong—nobody knew the whole story—and he left the company. What happened?

Larry was a mid-level manager who oversaw several sections. He knew about Wanda, the quiet wonder who gave her all to the company. She was a resource he guarded carefully, a flower that required just the right amount of praise and care. Conroy was another story. He interviewed well and should have been a great section manager. Unfortunately, he turned out to be a pest. Conroy got in just about everyone's good graces—but not Larry's. Larry was old school. You had to prove your worth through your work, and Conroy just wasn't delivering. Not his own work, anyway. Instead of helping his team, he used their ideas to promote himself. When Larry noticed Wanda was baking for Conroy, he knew something was up.

When Conroy presented the process improvements that eventually saved the company millions, Larry followed up behind the scenes with the truth. It was a hard sell, but others who'd been burned by Conroy came forward (not quiet Wanda, of course), and eventually they got rid of him.

The Herd

Danielle looked at the clock on the wall: 5:30. Well, we'll all be here until 6:00 tonight, she thought, and she pulled the next invoice from her stack and got back to work. There were about twenty clerks in the processing center. There had been twenty-five, but they lost five to budget cuts. At the last staff meeting, Mr. Gwaltmacher, their manager, told them that just because the girls were gone didn't mean their work was gone too; everyone would have to pitch in and get it done. Danielle dropped her right hand below her desk and shook it out. It was tingling and falling asleep again. Her body was taking a while to adjust to the longer days, but she'd be okay. Renee, to her right, let out a huge yawn. Phoebe, across from her, made a little "ahem," indicating they were all in this together so it was no use complaining. Sally announced, "A hundred to go," and there was a murmur of excitement. "Who's bringing tomorrow?" Gretchen asked. "Me," Danielle chirped. She made a quick note on a scrap of paper to pick up cookies. She felt bad that she wouldn't be bringing homemade cookies, but she'd be getting home later and just wouldn't have the time to bake. She hoped the girls wouldn't mind too much. What happened?

Nothing much happened. To meet their processing goals, the girls agreed to cut back on break time. They also found a few ways to improve the process, which saved some processing time. When the company started doing better, the five positions that were cut were never reopened because the processing center was keeping up with the work. Gwaltmacher got an efficiency bonus.

★ ★ ★ LLOYD "THE PARANOID POUNDER" ★ ★ ★

Alias: The Inquisitor, Paranoid.

Record: Mixed. Good record in the smaller bouts, but doesn't win the high-profile fights.

Division: Lightweight to Middleweight.

Reach: Limited.

Height: Lower levels of an organization, with occasional appearances in the upper levels.

Manager: Consuming fear of being taken advantage of or having weaknesses exposed created this boxer, who's quick to throw a punch.

★ ★ ★ ★ ★ ★

Fighter Profile

Lloyd's the guy who has his guard up before you even meet him. He doesn't trust anyone. Because he's always looking for an attack against him, he sees just about everything anyone does as a feint, a windup, or a punch. You compliment his tie, and he's offended because he just knows you're making fun of him. You disagree with him on how to resolve an office problem, and he treats you as if you punched him when he was down. He finds evidence in how you say hello, the number of times you go past (or don't go past) his desk—or even if you do something nice for him.

If you're on his good side, you only have to deal with his cold aloofness and biting sarcasm. He constantly checks to see if you are persecuting him, taking advantage of him, demeaning him, or trying to control him in some way. Whether he likes you or not, Lloyd will be critical of your work. Once he decides you are an opponent, he'll never tire in his quest to get you in the ring and pulverize you.

Although Lloyd can be an energetic, hard-working employee, it's never easy to get along with him. He carries grudges like real boxers carry titles: as long as he can. When he's made up his mind on an issue, he ignores or misinterprets any evidence to the contrary. He loves to prove other people's points wrong. He can be very quick to argue and often refuses to compromise.

Lloyd also refuses to accept blame or criticism. He trusts his judgment above any facts you can provide. His way is the best way, and if you try to get him to change, then you're infringing on his personal rights.

As you might guess, Lloyd doesn't make friends at the office, or anywhere, as far as you can tell. He's a definite loner. If you do talk to him, you'll see why: not many people can deal with his odd thoughts, weird fantasies, and peculiar language—in addition to his constantly suspicious nature.

Defense

Lloyd's main defense, keeping his guard up, is so good that he always sees the punch coming. As a matter of fact, he probably sees fifty imagined attacks for every real attack. Because he is under so many attacks (in his mind), he has developed lightning-fast responses.

He's also tireless. His belief that he is fighting the "good fight" (he's always right, always upholding some higher ideal, etc.) gives him energy to continue day after day, week after week, year after year. It doesn't take long for him to wear down most opponents.

Another aspect of Lloyd's defense is to keep a small corner. The fewer people in his corner, he figures, the fewer who will spill his weaknesses to the press or give him bad advice.

Offense

Lloyd has several good punches, and he doesn't hesitate to use them. His constant jabs help him determine if you are a threat. If he decides you are a threat, he will let loose with a lightning-quick cross that will knock you flat. If you get up, Lloyd will come at you again and again until he either feels vindicated or feels he has enough control over you that his area is safe once again.

If you throw a punch at him, as an attack or in defense, plan on a punishing counterpunch from Lloyd. He's not the kind of fighter to let anything slide; he will always try to get even.

Why Are You Fighting?

You might simply be standing around when Lloyd hauls off and pops you a good one. Odds are you thought you were on good-to-neutral terms with him. However, he thought:

- You criticized or made fun of him. This includes job reviews, feedback, and constructive criticism.
- You punished him—for example: docked his pay, demoted him, gave him a task he doesn't want.
- He perceives you as a person with authority over him who is abusing the authority by being domineering or taking away his autonomy.
- He feels threatened by you—for example: your career is advancing faster, or you have better connections.
- He feels he's been wronged and wants revenge.
- He feels he's been wronged and needs to show you that you can't get away with it.
- He wants to prove or make you admit that you're wrong—and he's right.
- Somehow, somewhere, you fit into one of his conspiracy theories—as an opponent, of course.

In the Ring

Believe it or not, Lloyd sometimes looks like Alex "the Great" at first glance. If you aren't sure who you're facing, give him a small compliment. If he takes it well, you probably have Alex; if he's suspicious, you probably have Lloyd.

If it's Lloyd, be mindful of your actions, weigh what you say before speaking, and tread lightly. For this fighter you need to use strategy. Because Lloyd can come across as a bit of a goofball, your gut feeling is that you can take him easily enough. But Lloyd is in it for the long haul, and once you throw a punch he won't stop fighting until he dominates you. Your best move is to get out of the ring. First, find out what he believes you did to him (it's highly doubtful you can figure it out yourself).

- If he thinks you criticized him:
  - Explain the circumstances.
  - If you criticized him as part of a review or feedback, go over the review again. Accentuate the positives; downplay the negatives.
  - Suggest that he file a grievance or complaint if he feels the process or the criticism is unfair. Note: do not help in any way with this, other than making the suggestion or giving him listed contact numbers—make sure he does it on his own.

- If he thinks you blamed him:
  - Explain the circumstances.
  - Offer to publicly apologize if you were in the wrong in the least.
  - Discuss how the situation can be avoided in the future.
  - Suggest that he file a grievance or complaint if he feels the issue has not been adequately addressed. Again, be supportive of his right to file a complaint, but make sure he does the work himself. Otherwise he'll think you're trying to trick him.

- If he thinks you are trying to control him and you're his:
  - Manager. Explain that you like your workers to have as much independence as possible, but that you also have to ensure everyone does their job satisfactorily. Discuss how much leeway he can have. Be very specific; for example, discuss latitude on each task.

- Co-worker. Explain that you know you're not his manager and that you're just trying to do the best job you can for the company. Discuss the circumstances, and determine how the situation can be avoided in the future.
- Subordinate. Apologize and explain you're just trying to do the best job you can for him and for the company. Discuss the circumstances, and determine how the situation can be avoided in the future.

■ If he thinks you took his idea or work and claimed it as your own:
- Explain the circumstances.
- If you did take his idea or work, apologize to him and offer to publicly apologize.
- Discuss how the situation can be avoided in the future.
- Suggest that he file a complaint if he feels the issue has not been adequately addressed.

■ If he thinks you aren't loyal:
- Explain the circumstances.
- Assure him you are loyal to him; his goals are your goals.

■ If he thinks you made fun of him:
- Explain the circumstances.
- Tell him that while you sometimes tell jokes, you try not to offend anyone.
- Apologize, either for the joke or the miscommunication.
- Suggest that he file a complaint if he feels the issue has not been adequately addressed.

■ If he is angry for another reason:
- Explain the circumstances.
- Apologize if necessary.
- Discuss how the situation can be avoided in the future.
- Suggest that he file a grievance or complaint if he feels the issue has not been adequately addressed.

If you can't get out of the ring—or you suddenly realize you're in the ring because you just got belted—roll with the punches coming your way and continue trying to get out, using the strategies above. If Lloyd is hammering away at you and shows no signs of letting up, try arbitration. Let him pick the neutral arbitrator. Tell management about the situation immediately. At the most they will step in to referee, but at least they will know about the fight and won't be blindsided if it escalates to a legal suit.

If you just couldn't help it and took a poke at Lloyd, keep your defense up and bring a doctor to your corner. Lloyd won't stop fighting until he gets revenge.

Ring Tips

- There is no "safe" topic of conversation with Lloyd. If he's of a mind to, he'll take affront at the most innocent comment. The best strategy is to be honest and straightforward with him. Even if you do so, he will still drag you into the ring. Try to keep to your strategy instead of pulling back and avoiding him. That will only make the situation worse.

- Lloyd is more hypersensitive and even quicker to the punch when he is stressed out. Roadblocks, setbacks, and new processes or equipment can really put him on edge. The more upset he is, the more dangerous he is.

- Being around Lloyd and his continual paranoia will drain your energy. Keep out of his area as much as possible. Remind yourself that it's him, not you.

- Lloyd bends all evidence to support his viewpoint. He does this even when it's obvious that he's wrong or it's clear that the problem is a direct consequence of his own actions. For example, if he was supposed to take the company car to the mechanic but didn't and then it broke down, making him miss a deadline, he will believe that it was the company's fault, mechanic's fault, the road condition, or even the car manufacturer's fault. But it was not his fault.

- Lloyd tends to think that all events are related to him. If the copy machine repairman is late, it isn't because traffic is bad but because he doesn't want Lloyd to meet his deadline. If the fire alarm goes off and it was a false alarm, it wasn't a faulty circuit but an espionage tactic to clear the building so a spy could get into his desk and files.

- Always act as though you are being taped, because Lloyd is the kind of guy who will install surveillance equipment. He's also the kind of guy who records (to the second) when you arrive, take your breaks, and leave. Be especially careful if Lloyd is in a position to monitor and fire employees.

- Try to give Lloyd choices instead of just giving him orders. For example, if work needs to be done by Monday, ask him if he'd rather stay late Friday or work on Saturday or Sunday instead of telling him he has to come in Saturday.

- Because Lloyd is paranoid, just about anything you do will make him think you're up to something. Since he'll probably complain to your boss (or the union, or take you to court), sometimes the only move you have is to beat him to the punch: tell him to complain to your boss (or the union or his lawyer). When you suggest that he complain if he is not happy with something, make sure of two things. First, be supportive. For example, say, "Your job description says there will be some weekend work. If you didn't know this, or if you feel you shouldn't have to be on call, the place to go is to the personnel office." Don't say, "Tough luck, it's in your job description. If you don't like it, call somebody who cares." Second, don't help. If you do, Lloyd will think you're setting him up by sending him to a specific person who you are secretly in league with to fire Lloyd.

- Don't use Lloyd to get back at someone else (see Hooks in Basic Skills). There's a very high probability that Lloyd will figure it out, and then he will put you in a world of hurt.

Matchups

If Lloyd is your manager, you'll do well enough as long as you don't wilt under his constant scrutiny and are able to continually prove your loyalty. Over-communicate new developments, rumors, and your upcoming plans. Explain any absences, changes in your regular routine, and breaks from the corporate norm. Make sure he knows that, as far as you're concerned, he's in command. His goals are your goals. Your wins are his wins. Mold your ambition to fit his needs or hide it from him—otherwise he'll think you're after his job. Lloyd gives praise sparingly to loyal hard workers. He dumps hate and rage on those who betray or disappoint him.

If Lloyd is your co-worker, take him seriously, avoid criticizing him, and communicate as sincerely as possible with him. Never make fun of him—not on April Fool's, not on his birthday, not ever. If he has a complaint about something you do, take it seriously. If you have issues with his work, try to discuss it with him; play up what you like, play down what you don't. If he won't budge, let him know that you have to bring the matter to his manager and ask if he would like to be there when you discuss it. He'll say yes. In team efforts, allow him to work as independently as possible. Always make sure his contributions are noted. Build a feeling of cooperation. If he attacks or passes blame onto you, let his manager know what is going on and that you are trying to resolve it at your level. With Lloyd, discuss the situation without criticizing him. Don't get into a debate.

If you supervise Lloyd, with the right handling he can be an excellent worker. Let him work as independently as possible. Keep the relationship on a business level; don't ask about his personal life or tell him about yours, and keep things cordial but impersonal and to the point. It would be helpful to let the entire office know that you don't condone making fun of workers. In general, keep Lloyd informed of changes in a friendly, non-threatening way. Explain why there are changes, and be specific when you describe the new method. Use the same format—explain why, be specific, keep things as non-threatening as possible—when you give him feedback. He will probably be offended no matter what you say or do. He takes criticism very hard, so be ready to spend extra time going over what he does well in addition to where he needs to make improvements. Before things get out of hand and he threatens to call the union or an attorney, suggest he take those steps if he feels it's necessary. Let management know if he threatens a lawsuit so they're prepared.

Fight Commentaries

Maxwell Hammers Joan

Maxwell "the Hatchet Man" managed a group of therapists. One of his subordinates, Joan, was a thorn in his side. She did not follow the time rules. She was almost always five minutes late coming in, took off for lunch two or three minutes early, and sometimes went several minutes over on her breaks. She was praised by her clients and her peers, and she got her work done, sometimes staying past quitting time. But that did not excuse her from following the office rules, in Maxwell's point of view. During a weekly individual status meeting, he told Joan that she must follow the rules. Three months later she was fired. What happened?

Joan didn't really believe Maxwell was serious. What were a few minutes here and there, especially when she got all her work done with no complaints? She watched the clock a little more closely after her meeting with Maxwell but fell into her regular habits a few weeks later. At a review board meeting about a month and a half later, Maxwell made a presentation about Joan's tardiness and asked for her dismissal. She couldn't believe the file he had on her. He must have been practically stalking her to get details like that. She tried to explain to the board that he was nit-picking, but in the end they sided with him. She tried to appeal the decision, but the organization let her go. She was told later that they had hated to see her go, but Maxwell was adamant that she was a poor employee and a bad example to others. He wouldn't rest—or let anyone else rest either—until she was gone.

Jack and his Beans

Jack was an accountant. He was a good worker and kept the books up to date and clean. During a time of cutbacks, he started to suspect that some marketing people were padding their expense reports. He tried rejecting some of the items on Donna's report, but she got Li, their boss, to back her. Just the way it was handled made Jack even more suspicious. He scrutinized all of Donna's reports from then on but could never catch her in a lie. He was sure, however, that she was padding her reports. He decided that the only way to get evidence of her stealing was to bug her work cube. He was also able to put in a small surveillance camera nearby so he would know when she was in the office and working on her reports.

Because his surveillance of Donna took time out of his week, he put in extra hours to get his own work done. He billed this as overtime. When Li asked him about his overtime, Jack explained he was spending more time on the expense reports. Li asked for more details and decided Jack needed to talk to Human Resources about employee privacy. Jack ended up suing the company (he lost) and then leaving just before he got fired. What happened?

Li told Tom in HR about the situation. Tom had a pretty good idea he was dealing with a paranoid pounder. At the first meeting between Jack and Tom, Jack asked if their conversations were going to be recorded. Tom said there were no cameras or tape recorders in his office as far as he knew, but that he couldn't be 100 percent sure. Someone could have put some type of device in the room, but that would have been without his knowledge or consent. Jack started to discuss expense reports, but Tom stopped him. He asked if Jack was really concerned about being taped. Jack said he was. Tom suggested that Jack should get a lawyer to draw up a contract that anything said in the room would not be knowingly recorded, taped, or otherwise conveyed to anyone else. Jack asked if Tom had such a form. Tom said there were forms he could get, but it would be best for Jack to get a lawyer he trusted to write up something airtight. Jack liked the suggestion and decided he would do that. In the meantime, however, he told Tom his side of the expense report story. Tom explained to Jack that he had violated Donna's privacy. Tom showed Jack the exact rules he had broken.

Jack argued his point, but Tom refused to budge. Tom told Jack that he would have to remove the surveillance equipment and follow the company's accounting rules, without embellishing them. Jack removed the equipment. Word got out about what he had done, and people started to talk and make jokes about him. Jack sued the company for having a hostile work environment. He continued to work there through the court case and an appeal and then left when he was forced into arbitration—he knew the arbitrator was on the company's side.

★ ★ ★ BOXING HIERARCHY ★ ★ ★

It's possible that any of the boxers described in this book can be found at any level in an organization. However, it's more likely you will find them in the areas they naturally gravitate toward.

Management and Leadership

- Alex the Great will always be fighting his way to the top. He works hard. He wants the respect and rewards of success, and he makes sure that he gets them.

- Mark the Machine gets things done. He follows orders and rules with no back talk. He's a natural for middle management.

- Lloyd the Paranoid Pounder needs to be in control of people and things. His dedication and control have earned him a spot in middle management.

Special Operations

- Katy the Chaos Kid arrives in a whirlwind of activity and has a great reputation. Things start to fall apart, and that's about when Katy flies off to something new.

- Conrad the Con Man is the right guy for whatever it is you need. (He prefers to be needed in a management position.) He's got ideas, he gets people to get things done, and then he's out the door, by hook or by crook.

Workers

- Faith the Phantom is a quiet workhorse who doesn't want anything to do with people. She's happiest being left alone to churn out her work.

- Sam the Saboteur sometimes makes his way up to lower management but generally limits himself to the lower ranks by undermining any good work he does with a bad attitude and mediocre performance.

- Stella the Belle wants to be liked too much to last in management, yet she's not detail-oriented enough to be a good worker. Luckily she has a creative flare that usually wins her a niche job spot. She comes to the office to socialize (and do some work).

- Nora the Needy Gnat needs—craves—someone to tell her what to do. With just the right kind of close supervision, she can be an okay worker.

- Gil the Nice Guy doesn't have enough self-confidence (or people skills) to manage others. He wants to come in and do the work that's needed to please his boss and company.

The Crowd

When boxers fight, who does the crowd get behind? In most cases, it's the person they unconsciously perceive to be the most powerful. Alex, Lloyd, Katy, and Conrad exude power and control, which is why they have so many people in their corners.

A few people will get behind a good guy "White Hat." They might feel sympathy for someone on the losing side. And they might get in a righteous mood and back a whistle blower. But if their fighter loses, they almost always alter their allegiance and back the winner.

Watch for this and remember it. If you need the crowd in your fight, you need to at least appear to be stronger than your opponent. If you know you don't have the crowd, you can win their allegiance (not necessarily their hearts) by winning the fight.

Having the crowd's allegiance because you are a powerful, ruthless fighter only works in the short run. In the long run it will wear them down, and they will gradually leave.

★ ★ ★ HISTORIC BOXING RULES ★ ★ ★

Broughton's Boxing Rules of 1743

1. That a square of a yard be chalked in the middle of the stage, and on every fresh set-to after a fall, or being parted from the rails, each Second is to bring his Man to the side of the square, and place him opposite to the other, and till they are fairly set-to at the Lines, it shall not be lawful for one to strike at the other.

2. That, in order to prevent any Disputes, the time a Man lies after a fall, if the Second does not bring his Man to the side of the square, within the space of half a minute, he shall be deemed a beaten Man.

3. That in every main Battle, no person whatever shall be upon the Stage, except the Principals and their Seconds, the same rule to be observed in bye-battles, except that in the latter, Mr. Broughton is allowed to be upon the Stage to keep decorum, and to assist Gentlemen in getting to their places, provided always he does not interfere in the Battle; and whoever pretends to infringe these Rules to be turned immediately out of the house. Every body is to quit the Stage as soon as the Champions are stripped, before the set-to.

4. That no Champion be deemed beaten, unless he fails coming up to the line in the limited time, or that his own Second declares him beaten. No Second is to be allowed to ask his man's Adversary any questions, or advise him to give out.

5. That in bye-battles, the winning man to have two-thirds of the Money given, which shall be publicly divided upon the Stage, notwithstanding any private agreements to the contrary.

6. That to prevent Disputes, in every main Battle the Principals shall, on coming on the Stage, choose from among the gentlemen present two Umpires, who shall absolutely decide all Disputes that may arise about the Battle; and if the two Umpires cannot agree, the said Umpires to choose a third, who is to determine it.

7. That no person is to hit his Adversary when he is down, or seize him by the ham, the breeches, or any part below the waist: a man on his knees to be reckoned down.

As agreed by several Gentlemen at Broughton's Ampitheatre, Tottenham Court Road, August 16, 1743.

The Marquis of Queensberry Rules

Written in 1865 by John Graham Chambers, member of the Amateur Athletic Club. Published in 1867, with the patronage of John Sholto Douglas, the eighth Marquis of Queensberry.

1. To be a fair stand-up boxing match, in a twenty-four foot ring, or as near that size as practicable.
2. No wrestling or hugging allowed.
3. The rounds to be of three minutes' duration, and one minute's time between rounds.
4. If either man falls through weakness or otherwise, he must get up unassisted, ten seconds to be allowed him to do so, the other man meanwhile to return to his corner, and when the fallen man is on his legs the round is to be resumed, and continued until the three minutes have expired. If one man fails to come to scratch in the ten seconds allowed, it shall be in the power of the referee to give his award in favor of the other man.
5. A man hanging on the ropes in a helpless state, with his toes off the ground, shall be considered down.
6. No seconds or any other person to be allowed in the ring during the rounds.
7. Should the contest be stopped by any unavoidable interference, the referee to name the time and place as soon as possible for finishing the contest; so that the match must be won and lost, unless the backers of both men agree to draw the stakes.
8. The gloves to be fair-sized boxing gloves of the best quality, and new.
9. Should a glove burst, or come off, it must be replaced to the referee's satisfaction.

10. A man on one knee is considered down, and if struck is entitled to the stakes.
11. No shoes or boots with springs allowed.
12. The contest in all other respects to be governed by the revised rules of the London Prize Ring.

★ ★ ★ GLOSSARY OF TERMS ★ ★ ★

The first definition is for boxing as a sport (1); the second applies to office boxing (2). (A second definition is not provided if not applicable.)

Bantamweight. See Weight Classes.

Bell. 1. Signal denoting the start and end of a round. 2. Direction from management to "stop fighting" or to "get along" with your opponent.

Boxing. 1. The sport of fighting with the fists. 2. The strategy of office survival.

Blocking. 1. Defending against a punch by deflecting it with your gloves, arms, shoulders, etc. 2. Defending against an attack by deflecting its intensity or validity.

Blow. 1. Punch, hit. 2. An attack.

Butt. 1. Use of head or shoulder in hitting the opponent. Butts are fouls. 2. Use of dirty tricks to hurt others.

Cauliflower ear. 1. An ear deformed by repeated blows. 2. A person's spirit broken by repeated attacks.

Clinch. 1. Embrace (lock arms) to immobilize an opponent's arms. 2. To immobilize an opponent from taking a particular action.

Combination punch. 1. A sequence of punches thrown without pause, usually starting and ending with a jab. 2. A sequence of offensive moves.

Counterpunch. 1. Punch thrown after the opponent's lead punch. Also, a strategy to wait until the opponent is committed to throwing a punch and then throwing your own. 2. Response to an attack.

Crowd. 1. Audience. 2. Co-workers.

Cudgeling. 1. Boxing.

Defense. 1. Use of blocks, footwork, and strategy to avoid taking or to minimize the effect of blows. 2. Use of blocks, footwork, and strategy to reduce the number or to minimize the effect of attacks from others.

Diet. 1. Food intake. 2. Compliment and complaint intake.

Elbowing. 1. Use of elbows to hit the opponent. Elbowing is a foul. 2. Unethical or illegal action.

Featherweight. See Weight Classes.

Fisticuffs. 1. Fighting, boxing.

Flick. 1. Hitting the opponent with an open glove. Flicking is a foul. 2. Unethical or illegal action.

Flyweight. See Weight Classes.

Footwork. 1. The movement of your feet while boxing. Ability to move in such a way that your opponent is backed into the ropes or a corner. Positioning yourself to attack or counter an attack 2. The movement in, around, and out of conversations.

Foul. 1. An infraction of the rules. 2. Unethical or illegal action.

Guard. 1. Defense. 2. Defense.

Heavyweight. See Weight Classes.

Hook. 1. Punch thrown with your arm at a 90-degree angle and parallel to the floor. Hooks are usually aimed at the side of the opponent's head or torso. 2. An indirect attack that the opponent doesn't usually see coming.

Jab. 1. Fast punch thrown from the front arm. The jab is usually used to determine timing and reach but can also cause damage. 2. Setting boundaries, determining your opponent's strategy.

Jumping Rope. 1. Exercise with a jump rope to improve stamina, coordination, and footwork. 2. Mental exercise to improve ability to think (including how to react) during an attack.

Knockout. 1. A blow that causes unconsciousness. The act of knocking out an opponent. 2. Successfully defending yourself against an attack. Getting your opponent removed (fired, transferred) from your work area.

KO. See Knockout.

Lightweight. See Weight Classes.

Middleweight. See Weight Classes.

Pugilism. 1. Boxing.

Punch. 1. Hit. 2. Attack. Move offensively against an opponent.

Punch yourself out. 1. Throw so many punches in the early stages of the fight that you run out of energy and your later punches have no power. 2. Misjudge your opponent in that your offensive moves are not sufficient. Use all your offensive moves up before the attack is over.

Punching bag. 1. Equipment used for practicing punches. 2. A person who an unethical fighter attacks when the primary target is not available or is too dangerous to attack.

Ring. 1. A raised platform enclosed by ropes where boxers fight. 2. Any place (at work or away from it) where you are in the company of co-workers.

Ring talk. 1. Talk between a fighter and the people in his corner (pep talk) or his opponent (trash talk). 2. Talk between you and your opponent (before, during, and after an attack).

Roadwork. 1. Running. 2. Stress reduction.

Round card beauty. 1. Scantily clad woman who tells the audience which round the fight is in by strutting across the ring while holding a large card with the round number on it.

Shadow boxing. 1. Practicing throwing combinations in front of a mirror. 2. Practicing fighting in a non-fight environment.

Spoiler. 1. Fighter who isn't among the top fighters in his weight category but who can make a good fighter look bad. 2. Opponent who doesn't fight often but can be devastating when he does fight.

Stance. 1. Position of the feet while throwing a punch. 2. Physical demeanor. Body language.

Stretching. 1. Warming up muscles. 2. Making contacts among co-workers.

Sucker punch. 1. A blow made without warning, allowing no time for preparation or defense on the part of the recipient. It is usually delivered from close range or from behind. Sucker punches are illegal. 2. An attack from an unexpected source, such as a supposed friend.

Take a dive. 1. Intentionally lose a fight, usually for monetary compensation. 2. Intentionally lose the fight, usually for survival (continued employment) purposes.

Technical knockout. 1. When a fight is awarded to a boxer because the referee has determined the opponent is either too injured to continue or is taking too much punishment. 2. When a boxer has for all intents and purposes defeated his opponent's attack.

Tie up. See Clinch.

TKO. See Technical knockout.

Weight classes. 1. Divisions that fighters are divided into based on their weight. The seven major divisions, from heaviest to lightest, are: heavyweight, middleweight, welterweight, lightweight, featherweight, bantamweight, and flyweight. 2. How far up in the company organization you will find the fighter, matching weight classes from heaviest (highest) to lightest (lowest).

Welterweight. See Weight Classes.

★ ★ ★ RESOURCES ★ ★ ★

The following resources were used during research for this book:

Acunto, Stephen. *Champions Boxing Guide.* New York: CCG Publishing, Inc, 1996. Print.

American Heritage Dictionary. New York: Dell Publishing Co, 1984. Print.

Cavaiola, Alan, PhD, and Neil Lavender, PhD. *Toxic Coworkers: How to Deal with Dysfunctional People on the Job.* Oakland, CA: New Harbinger Publications, 2000.

Gabarro, John, and John Kotter. "Managing Your Boss." Harvard Business Review, *Best of HBR 1980.* Print.

Gibbon, Miriam; Robert Spitzer; and Andrew Skodol. *DSM-IV Casebook: A Learning Companion to the Diagnostic and Statistical Manual of Mental Disorders.* Virginia: American Psychiatric Publishing, Inc., 1994. Print.

Haden Elgin, Suzette, PhD. *Success with the Gentle Art of Verbal Self-Defense.* New Jersey: Prentice Hall, 1989. Print.

Hare, Robert, PhD. *Without Conscience: The Disturbing World of the Psychopaths Among Us.* New York: Pocket Books, 1993. Print.

HickockSports. Early Boxing (to 1838). Web. <http://www.hickoksports.com/history/boxing01.shtml>

Johnson, Stephen, MD. *Character Styles.* New York: WW Norton & Company, 1994. Print.

Mason, Paul, and Randi Kreger. *Stop Walking on Eggshells: Taking Your Life Back When Someone You Care About Has Borderline Personality Disorder.* Oakland, CA: New Harbinger Publications, 2010.

McWilliams, Nancy, PhD, and Stanley Lependorf, PhD. *Narcissistic Pathology of Everyday Life: The Denial of Remorse and Gratitude.* Institute for Psychoanalysis and Psychotherapy of New Jersey. <http://www.ippnj.org/mcwilliams1.html>

Oates, Joyce Carol. *On Boxing.* New York: Harper Perennial Modern Classics. 2006. Print.

Pacheco, Ferdie. *The 12 Greatest Rounds of Boxing: The Untold Stories.* Toronto: SportClassic Books, 2003. Print.

Scott, Danna. *Boxing: The Complete Guide to Training and Fitness.* New York: Perigee Trade, 2000. Print.

Stout, Martha, PhD. *The Sociopath Next Door.* New York: Broadway Books, 2005. Print.

Made in the USA
Lexington, KY
18 December 2012